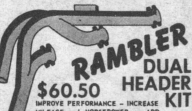

I looked in the mirror and a red light was blinkin'—
The cops was after my Hot Rod Lincoln.
Well, they arrested me and put me in jail.
I called my pop to make my bail;
He said, "Son, you're gonna drive me to drinkin',
If you don't quit drivin' that Hot Rod Lincoln!"

—Charlie Ryan, "Hot Rod Lincoln," 1955

"What's the use of hopping up a car if you can't give her the gun?"

—Teenaged hot rodder Darryl Hickman, *The Devil on Wheels*, 1947

Speed! It had a good smell and a pretty sound. You taste it . . . hear it sing while you watched things streak by and felt the heart-tripping chill of it sometimes on close shaves to your bones. Then the deep breath and you were with-it. Really living it up. And life was swift and worth the risk.

—Edward De Roo, *Go, Man, Go!*, 1959

AUTO RACES

Fastest Cars - In Central California - Best Drivers

EVERY SUNDAY
AFTERNOON Time Trials Start 1 P.M.

WATSONVILLE

PALM BEACH SPEEDWAY
BEACH ROAD - 3 MILES WEST

Cars Sponsored by Central California Racing Association

WATSONVILLE PRESS 119 WALL STREET

1950 HOT ROD AND **MOTOR SPORTS SHOW**

Sponsored by
RUSSETTA TIMING ASSOCIATION

LOS ANGELES National Guard Armory

HOLLISTER ROD KNOCKERS

Carrell Speedway

Presents

HOT ROD RACES

SANCTIONED BY C.R.A.

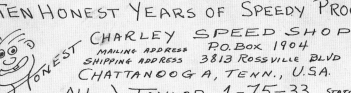

10th ANNIVERSARY 1948=1958

TEN HONEST YEARS OF SPEEDY PROGRESS

HONEST CHARLEY SPEED SHOP

MAILING ADDRESS P.O. Box 1904
SHIPPING ADDRESS 3813 Rossville Blvd
CHATTANOOGA, TENN., U.S.A.

LOOKOUT MOUNTAIN AND ROCK CITY ARE IN OUR SHADOW

ALL PHONES ▷ TAYLOR 1-75-33 STATION TO STATION

$AVE $$$ PHONE STATION TO STATION — NO ONE
WILL ANSWER THAT CANNOT ANSWER YOUR
QUESTIONS AND TAKE YOUR ORDER

HELLO!

A CHANGE HAS BEEN MADE IN 10 YEARS

1948   1958

$100 FREE

1958 EDITION 25¢ TO COVER MAILING AND HANDLING COST

CERTIFICATE   SEE INSIDE BACK COVER

SUPRISE MONEY SAVER CATALOG

NOTICE: ALL PRICES SUBJECT TO CHANGE WITHOUT NOTICE — BEING IN POSSESSION
OF THIS CATALOG DOES NOT CONSTITUTE A GIVEN RIGHT TO PURCHASE AT PRICES STATED
ALL SPECIFICATIONS ARE SUBJECT TO CHANGE WITHOUT NOTICE
ANY PRINCIPAL OR POLICY ENCOMPASSED HEREIN IS NOT TO BE CONSTRUED AS FOOLPROOF
NOR WILL WE BE HELD LIABLE FOR ANY UNUSUAL RESULT FROM USE OF ITEMS HEREIN.

NO RETURNS WITHOUT OUR PERMISSION AT ANY TIME
10% HANDLING CHARGE ON ALL RETURNS MADE IN 15 DAYS
NO RETURNS AFTER 15 DAYS (EXCEPT WITH SPECIAL PERMISSION)
25% HANDLING CHARGE ON RETURNS AFTER MORE THAN 15 DAYS

NO C.O.D.'s UNDER $5.00

ALL RETURNS MUST BE PREPAID TO US
IF YOU SEND IT C.O.D.
OR COLLECT WE WILL
REFUSE IT AND YOU
WILL PAY BOTH WAYS

WE SHIP BY — GENERAL PARCEL POST RAILWAY EXPRESS   AIR EXPRESS AIR FREIGHT   TRUCK

BY BUS — TO LIMITED STATIONS — WITHIN 250 MILE RADIUS
AND ONLY ON THOSE THAT CARRY C.O.D. OR COLLECT PACKAGES.

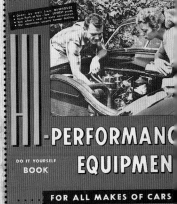

S.C.T.A.
Speed Trials
PROGRAM

El Mirage Time Trials
May 6-7, 1950   25¢

Southern California Timing Association, Inc.

OFFICIAL PROGRAM

JULY 24 1949   25¢

RUSSETTA *timing* ASSOCIATION, INC.

S. C. T. A

SOUTHERN CALIFORNIA TIMING ASSOCIATION

"SPONSORS OF THE WORLD'S *Safest* AUTOMOTIVE SPEED TRIALS"

RACEITORIAL

APRIL 1968

Russetta

Safety Fast

TIMING ASSOCIATION

Cruisin', lookin' for my gal,
I'm cruisin', goin' don't know where . . .

—Gene Vincent, "Cruisin'," 1957

Toolin' down the highway doin' 79,
I'm a twin-pipe papa and I'm feelin' fine!

—Nervous Norvus, "Transfusion," 1956

When he was behind the wheel, in control of his hopped-up motor, he was king of the road. When he was happy, his happiness reached its peak when he could express it in terms of speed and roaring power, the pull of his engine, the whistle of the wind in his ears, and the glorious sensation of free flight. When he was unhappy, discontented, moody, the wheel again offered him his answer. At these times there was solace and forgetfulness behind the wheel. The motor snarled rather than sang, speed became a lance rather than a banner, and revenge against trouble was won through the conquest of other cars that accepted his challenge to race. And when he was alone on the road, his car and its speed seemed to remove him from the troubles that plagued him while his feet had contact with the earth.

— Henry Gregor Felsen, *Hot Rod,* 1950

The Ford was a straight-stick and she took it away in second. The motor screamed, reached its peak and at seventy she snapped it into high. The dual carbs sucked greedily at the air and gas and the tachometer on the steering column moved beyond the 4500 r.p.m. mark, wavered briefly and then continued its upward climb. Seconds later she threw it into overdrive and the Ford began to devour the vacant highway the way a hungry cow eats grass.

—Charles Verne, *Mr. Hot Rod,* 1957

It was not by any means the neatest and smoothest looking street rod in the world, but it was a pretty snazzy automotive creation by a seventeen-year-old youth, and as far as Jerry was concerned he wouldn't have traded it for a couple of brand-new Cadillacs.

—Robert Sidney Bowen, *Hot Rod Fury,* 1963

They are freedom, style, sex, power, motion, color—everything is right there.

—Tom Wolfe, *The Kandy-Kolored Tangerine-Flake Streamline Baby,* 1965

THE ALL-AMERICAN

HOT ROD

The Cars. The Legends. The Passion.

Michael Dregni, Editor. With stories, photographs, and artwork from Robert Williams, Henry Gregor Felsen, Gale Banks, Pat Ganahl, Albert Drake, David Fetherston, Steve Hendrickson, Allan Girdler, Budd Davisson, Kent Bash, Brad Bowling, Jay Carnine, Vince Crain, Peter Tytla, Dale Klee, and more.

Voyageur Press

ACKNOWLEDGMENTS

Special praise is due to David Fetherston and Pat Ganahl for their timely and committed work on this project.

My thanks to everyone else involved, in alphabetical order: Gale Banks and Joyce Macormac at Gale Banks Engineering; Kent Bash; Tom Benford; Brad Bowling; Jay Carnine; Vince Crain; Budd Davisson; Albert Drake; Karen Felsen; Allan Girdler; Steve Hendrickson; Henry Highrise; Dale Klee; Chuck Klein; Roy Newton; Don Pennington; Peter Tytla; and, last but not least, Robert Williams.

Edited by Michael Dregni

Designed by Julie Vermeer

Printed in China

04   05   06   07   08   5   4   3   2   1

Library of Congress Cataloging-in-Publication Data

The all-American hot rod : the cars, the legends, the passion / Michael Dregni, editor.
   p. cm.
 ISBN 0-89658-654-5 (hardcover)
 1. Hot rods--United States. I. Dregni, Michael, 1961-
 TL236.3.A25 2005
 629.228'6--dc22

2004014319

Distributed in Canada by Raincoast Books, 9050 Shaughnessy Street, Vancouver, B.C. V6P 6E5

Published by Voyageur Press, Inc., 123 North Second Street, P.O. Box 338, Stillwater, MN 55082 U.S.A.
651-430-2210, fax 651-430-2211 | books@voyageurpress.com | www.voyageurpress.com

Permissions: Portions of "My Old Hot Rod" first appeared in *California Hot Rodder* by Jay Carnine. Copyright © 2000 by Jay Carnine. They are reprinted by permission of the author and Graffiti Publications Pty. Ltd.

The essays "Surf Rods" and "A Portrait of the Artist as a Young Hot Rodder" first appeared in the *Rodder's Journal*. They are reprinted by permission of the author and the *Rodder's Journal*.

ON THE ENDSHEETS: Classic advertisements from the golden years of hot rodding.

ON PAGE 1: This is exactly how hot rodding started—an old, inexpensive roadster rebuilt in the backyard with whatever parts a pioneering hot rodder could scrounge. (Pat Ganahl collection)

ON PAGE 2: The chromed front end of Scott Mazes' '27 track roadster is slick and simple with its Model A spring, tube shocks, dropped axle, Chevy Corvair steering box, '40 Ford spindles, and modified finned brake drums from a '66 Buick Riviera. (Photograph © David Fetherston)

ON PAGE 3: Hot rod details. (Photographs © David Fetherston)

ON PAGES 4 AND 5: Possibly the most famous of all hot rod paintings—artist Robert Williams' acrylic-on-board *Hot Rod Race*. (Artwork © Robert Williams)

ON PAGE 6, CLOCK-WISE FROM TOP: Following World War II and the boom in hot rodding, the Los Angeles Police Department declared war on what officials labeled the "hot rod menace." Tickets were issued to any car without fenders or with headlights less than 28 inches above the ground. Other instantly enacted "fix-it" laws could also result in fines. (Pat Ganahl collection)

Busted! A roadster driver's race with the law comes to an end in the Los Angeles River.

Poster from *Born to Speed*, a daredevil hot-rod racing movie from 1947.

ON PAGES 8 AND 9: Images of the all-American hot rod.

ON PAGES 10 AND 11: Early hot rodding race and show posters, decals, club insignia, newsletters, and speed shop catalogs.

ON PAGE 12: Early hot rodders and their rides.

ON PAGE 13: Lance Stanford wanted a classic '32 Hi-Boy roadster and so built this nostalgic rod. He used a So-Cal chassis with a step-boxed frame. The drivetrain is a 330-horsepower 350 Chevy crate motor. The body is from Wescott's and features a 2-inch chopped windshield with black primer paintwork. (Photograph © David Fetherston)

ON PAGES 14 AND 15: Hot rod and custom car club plaques.

ON TITLE PAGES: Comicbook artwork from *Hot Rods and Racing Cars,* Vol.1, No.29, January 1957,

ON FACING PAGE: In creating his modern-day images of outrageous hot-rodded cars, artist Vince Crain was inspired by the 1960s Rat Fink artwork of Ed "Big Daddy" Roth, drawings by Dave Deal, and *CARtoons* magazines. (Artwork © Vince Crain)

ON PAGE 208: "Hell Rod" screams "lock up your daughters, hide your children, and cover your eyes" as its lopes down the street. Mild-mannered John Shipp built his outrageous blown '32 Tudor with a sense of humor, meshing the wildest imaginings of an Ed Roth cartoon with the reality of building that image into a real hot rod. (Photograph © David Fetherston)

vince crain © 2003

Contents

Introduction

The All-American
HOT ROD

Facing page, **RAT ROD:**
Rat rodders still exist on
the edge of hot rodding
and still consider it a
lifestyle to drive unconven-
tional and extremely wild
machines. Roy Zamaripa is
one. His '37 Chevy pickup
"Smokin' 36s" rides a '41
Chevy pickup frame with
a channeled and chopped
cab, making the pickup's
roof sit nearly 5 feet lower
than its original height.
The body combination is a
modified '29 Ford pickup
bed, '37 Chevy truck cab,
and raked '36 Dodge grille
shell. Putting the poke in
this ride is a rebuilt '78
Chevy 350/383 four-bolt
small-block Chevy. (Photograph © David Fetherston)

It all began with a Big Bang.

For just a fraction of a second, there was an infinitely small, dense, hot fireball. Then, atoms of gases exploded and a primeval energy was unleashed. The force expanded at a rapid rate, pushing ever outward.

And thus, in the small universe of the combustion chamber, horsepower was born.

With power came the corruptive drive for more power. Carburetors were modified to flow more gas and air. New cams were ground, ignition systems advanced, headers designed, supercharging invented.

The Big Bang was now made bigger.

Bigger, of course, was better. It meant spinning the tires down Main Street, an extra ounce of speed on the dry lakes, a car's length in a drag race, and an exhaust note that rattled windows—not to mention shaking the nerves of the status quo.

It took a special kind of physicist to create and harness this Big Bang. They weren't scientists gowned in white lab coats running mathematical formulae or staring through telescopes. Instead, they were young men and women in grease-encrusted jeans and oily T-shirts working in garages, driveways, and under shade trees, learning as they made up the rules. As soon as the first two automobiles were built and met each other on a street, the drivers naturally had to see which machine was faster. And the loser likely became the first of a new breed—a spiritual hot rodder, seeking more horsepower in his mechanical steed.

Hot rodding truly started in the 1920s and 1930s in California, although the term hadn't been coined then. Cars were the craze, and young men and women could buy old Tin Lizzies on the cheap, strip off the fenders and the hood, hot up the engine, and have a machine that outperformed all the other cars on the street.

Hot rodding was born.

In the early days, they called them by the descriptive terms Soup-Ups, Gow Jobs, or Cut-Downs. The name Hot Rod came later, but it's the name that stuck—two words that police officers and parents said as a curse and that kids whispered with awe. And then came Customs, Rat Rods, Street Rods, and more. It was an all-American fad, this need for wheels and speed with an individual touch. And through the years, hot rodding became an Art with a capital "A."

Hot rods have made legends. They've been the ride of choice for James Dean and Edd "Kookie" Byrnes, Ricky Nelson and Dick Dale, Bud Crayne and John Milner. They were the soul of *Rebel without a Cause* and *American Graffiti*. They have also been at the heart of the development of rock'n'roll, inspiring countless love songs sung in their praise.

This book, then, is a different kind of history of the hot rod. It's not your typical scholarly and academic account packaged into a neat chronology of dates and places, trends and movements, movers and shakers. Hot rodding didn't happen that way. It was rarely neat and clean. Instead, it was a grassroots, groundswell movement, an underground artform that defies a straightforward chronicle succinctly tied up in a bow.

Thus, this book is a history told through numerous voices and images by people who were there making history. It's raw and disorderly, humorous and raucous, simple and yet complex. The authors include an array of famous hot rod historians and authors, a renowned artist, a beloved novelist, and several ordinary folk who simply love hot rods and have a good yarn to tell. Photographs, paintings, and illustrations come from a variety of respected automotive photographers and artists as well as the archives of numerous hot rodders. It's truly an all-American tale with an exhaust note heard 'round the world.

If you are still in awe of that first hot rod, still riding and wrenching on hot rods, or still dreaming hot rods, then this book is for you.

—Michael Dregni

CHAPTER 1

BEGINNINGS

It was a Jacob's coat of a car that Bud Crayne had built. The body had come off an old Ford coupe. Bud had sanded the original black finish and repainted with a dull red prime coat. Some day he intended to put on a finish coat.... The dual chrome exhaust pipes gave the first hint as to what might be found under the dull red hood. ... In contrast to the usual greasy motors found under gleaming hoods, the nondescript body of Bud's car concealed a motor that shone like a warship's brightwork on inspection day.

– Henry Gregor Felsen, *Hot Rod*, 1950

JALOPY RACE: A phalanx of hotted-up and stripped-down jalopies await the starting gun. Jalopy races in the 1920s and 1930s were the proving ground for early hot rodders.

HOT RODDING
in the Days before Nostalgia

By Allan Girdler

Allan Girdler's hobbies and career have been intertwined around engines and wheels. A former editor of *Car Life* and *Cycle World,* as well as an executive editor of *Road & Track,* Allan is also the author of an eclectic blend of books on motoring history, from cars to Harley-Davidson motorcycles.

In the beginning, it was hot rods that inspired Allan. Growing up in the Midwest, far from the flashpoints of hot rodding in Southern California, he still remembers the day he spotted his first hop-up and the brave new world it opened to him.

THE GOLDEN DAYS BEFORE NOSTALGIA: A group of hot rodders wrench on their rod in 1951.

"You see that exit? You drive down there and get off this highway. And if I ever see this car again . . ."

Keep those threatening words in mind while we flash back to the happy beginning.

It was 1950 and I was thirteen years old, waiting for the school bus in my small hometown when around the corner skittered a Ford roadster, bright blue with yellow wire wheels, stripped of fenders and hood, and equipped with two carburetors jutting above the hoodline and exhaust pipes sweeping out and down.

My future flashed before my eyes. I didn't know what I'd just seen but I did know, instantly, that that was what I was gonna do.

And I was in luck. My older brother had always been sensible and responsible. He'd mowed lawns and shoveled snow and minded kids, and when he graduated from high school he'd saved enough money for a year-old Ford convertible—with money left over for mild customizing and special paint, lime green if memory serves.

So when I was fourteen and I asked my dad when I could have a car, he naturally thought of my brother and said, "When you can buy one."

A Saturday or so later he wondered why I kept looking out the window.

"Walt's bringing me my car."

"Your car? What car?"

"His Model A. You said I could have a car when I could buy one, so I saved $50 and bought Walt's."

Dad paused for reflection, rubbed his chin and looked out the window.

"That wasn't what I meant. But it *is* what I said . . . OK, you can do it."

Keep in mind, this was the dawn of the 1950s. *Road & Track* and *Hot Rod* had barely made it to the newsstands, people stared at Volkswagens—never mind cut-down Fords; Chevrolet relied on the Stovebolt Six and Ford on the Flathead V-8, still overheating after twenty years in production; and Lee Petty was about to wreck the family Buick in the races.

Car nuts were few and far between, and blissfully ignorant.

In my favor, though, my dad's integrity aside, was that we lived in a small town, in a neighborhood developed by my great-grandfather in the previous century, which is to say we owned the roads around our house, so as soon as I mastered clutch, gas, and gearshift, I could hot-lap the neighborhood—OK, in first gear most of the time.

Plus, it was a short walk home. The car was twenty-one, I was now fourteen, and I got to walk home a lot. I knew little and my dad wasn't mechanically inclined, so when something broke or fell off I'd call the mechanic at the town's service (not gas, I mean *service*) station, who took car of our family car. I'd tell him what the sound was; he'd diagnose; I'd hitch into the city and buy the part, tool, or both; and I'd learn by doing.

My car was a future classic, a 1931 Model A Ford roadster, with dismountable windshield and side curtains, as distinguished from a convertible, which has a permanent windshield and windows that crank up and down.

My first acts were to take off the fenders, hood, running boards, bumpers, and top with a hammer and cold chisel. I painted the wheels with aluminum paint, sprayed from a can and they looked it. Rust revealed by the stripping was patched, sort of, with cloth mat and bondo, primed by spray can.

One fact lost to today's folklore is that back in the 1930s, when racers couldn't afford pure competition engines like Offenhausers and Millers, they went stock block. The dirt circuits were contested by modified Model A and B engines, with aluminum heads, overhead-valve conversions, and even overhead camshafts. The Ford V-8 wasn't the pioneer engine, and didn't become the focus of the sport until later.

This did me good. There was a small if brisk trade in used speed equipment for the fours, and I latched onto a two-carb manifold and Stromberg 97 carburetors, a high-compression cylinder head, and what we called a three-quarter-race camshaft, meaning it added power at the top of the rev range but still would start when cold.

I even found a set of exhaust headers that swept out and down to a muffler but with a cap—a "lakes plug," the magazines told us, which one removed when the power of straight pipes was called for—see *American Graffiti* for details.

Some of our collective—um, forgot to say most kids in this era would settle for the family sedan once a week. They thought we were loonies and wastrels, which I suppose we were.

But some of our ignorance was just that. Every week I'd buy copper tubing and compression gaskets and run a line from the fuel filter on the firewall to the line between the carbs. Every week the line would break.

After maybe two months of this, the guy at the parts store explained that the engine vibrated and the firewell didn't and the line was being fatigued. Make the line longer, he said, and wind a couple of gentle circles into it.

And it worked.

Stepping out of time for effect, one day I was driving my girl cousin into town. The sixty-pound flywheel came off the crankshaft, made a circuit inside the bellhousing, then burst out the bottom of the bellhousing, taking the transmission with it, and exploded on the pavement.

We coasted to a halt, trailing gear lube and bits of cast iron. I walked to the nearest house and called my brother to come push us home.

When I got back to the car, my cousin said, "Try it now. Maybe it's OK."

I looked down at the slurry of oil and iron, and said nothing.

And some of our ignorance was dangerous. I rolled out from beneath my brother's car, where I'd been whanging on the rear spring shackles so we could remove the axle, and gave the shackles one more whack—and was shocked to see the spring release with enough force to take a chunk out of the garage floor, right where my head had been.

Never occurred to me it supported half a ton.

But that's getting ahead of the story.

By the time I turned sixteen, the only birthday that's ever meant anything to me, as in Free At Last, I knew how cars worked. The driving test was no problem, not after all those laps of the neighborhood and well, yeah, I worked out a route of private roads, driveways, and vacant lots, crossing only a couple of public streets, that got me to the beach, as in I had wheels, ladies.

Except that a snapshot from that time shows me maybe five-feet-one, a hundred pounds, in my engineer boots, the face of a grinning teen barely able to see out of the car.

Every patrol car in my corner of that small state stopped me, once a day at least.

My license allowed me to expand my foolishness.

Hot Rod Magazine, which I read mostly while standing at the magazine rack of the stationary store, keeping an eye peeled for the owner, didn't spend much space on the past—well heck, hot rodding didn't have that much past, dry lakes excepted. There were drag strips, one in the east and one near Chicago, I read, and they printed the times, so I knew that my roadster, weighing less than 2,000 pounds and equipped with a healthy four-cylinder engine, would turn the standing quarter mile in fifteen seconds flat.

My peers, the other kids with souped-up Fords, didn't know that. All they read was the news about Flathead V-8s, with more power and more weight.

HAPPY HOT RODDER:
At the wheel of his first hot rod, author Allan Girdler sits like a king on his throne. He was just fourteen when this photo was shot, piloting his brother John and cousin Bill surreptitiously around the neighborhood. You don't need to know much about hot rods to see that Allan hadn't yet installed his souped-up engine or added his '32 grille. First things first: he removed useless stuff like fenders, running boards, and hood—gracefully using a hammer and cold chisel. (Allan Girdler collection)

Plus those kids hadn't been driving for a couple of years.

So I had the advantages of the hole shot, a term we didn't know yet, and of surprise, and I won a lot of root beer.

Speaking of surprise, a fifteen-second quarter-mile doesn't sound that quick now, but a review of the tests from the early 1950s turns up less performance from, oh, a Porsche Speedster, Jaguar XK-140, and Austin-Healey 100-S.

Trust me here, those tests were accurate, and weren't those sports car chaps astonished.

Nor did they necessarily feel any sort of kinship.

Going back in chronology here, before I got my license I was lucky enough to hitch a ride to the first road races at what was then Thompson Speedway in Connecticut.

One of the entries was a Miller-Ford, a two-place sprint car from the early 1930s, lovely car, thoroughbred lines and all that, but with an engine *just like mine!*

The owner couldn't get it to run right. 'Course at the age of fifteen I knew everything and stepped up to tell the guy I could fix it.

He turned me down, in words I'd been practicing but hadn't yet used in public.

Against that, back before nostalgia was invented and performance cars were a major market, there was a form of kinship. The kids, of course.

But my folks had friends in town, one of whom restored antique cars. Read *antiques*, as in an '07 Metz, if I remember correctly, with a variable-speed transmission.

I wasn't old enough to appreciate that era, and my guess would be my clapped old Ford wasn't his bag, either.

Except, his son was a pleasant youth who only cared about music, while my dad, as mentioned, viewed cars as the best way to get to the tennis courts.

One Saturday, Mr. and Mrs. Abbott (Horace Abbott, in case any of his children became interested in cars later) were visiting my folks. Mr. Abbott came out to the garage where I was tinkering, lakes plug uncapped.

"Do your parents have any idea how fast this car is?" he asked.

Pause for some thought. Mr. Abbott of course

knew exactly how fast it was. He also knew the brakes were marginal and the steering was worn, likewise the front suspension.

My childhood training took over.

"No."

Then he had to pause.

"I probably ought to tell 'em. But I won't."

Years later, when I knew a lot less than I knew when I was sixteen, it struck me that Mr. Abbott had hit on, or maybe knew, the best way to make me as responsible as a sixteen-year-old street racer could be.

It worked. Well, most of the time.

For instance, one night I was driving home from work and the car was running perfectly, the night was clear, and the road empty, and from someplace came the impulse to drop into first, let the engine idle . . . and climb out of the car.

There I was, as the fighter pilots say, walking along next to the car, one hand on the wheel . . .

The engine stumbled and caught, the car leaped forward, I lost my grip, and the left rear wheel ran over my foot.

Then there I was, hopping and howling until I realized the car was still ambling down the road, so I skipped and leaped and caught up, jumped in, and drove home, bruised and chastened, and even today I'm the only driver I know who's ever run over himself.

It must be true, as the poet says, 'cause there's no way I could have made that up.

Younger readers must keep in mind here that the kids and young men evolving the sport of hot rodding were able to do it only because we were not experimenting with classic treasures. There were classic and vintage cars back then, but they were Duesenbergs and Marmons and so forth, really old and large and complicated.

We were driving leftovers, clapped-out jalopies. Well, as another incident with a moral, a kid from the next town south called me one morning.

His car had broken down, again, and he needed a ride home, for the umpteenth time, and at dinner that night his dad laid down the law. The car was history. Get rid of it, no more, that's it.

I asked where it was and he said, up on the Post Road, near Pike's farm.

Not far from my home, so I said, "Give ya ten bucks for it."

"Done," he said.

Not much later, before I'd even begun to plan a haul home, I got a call from Skip, my friend from two towns to the north.

"McDougal's dad made him sell his car," I said, "and I bought it."

"Yeah?" said Skip. "Watcha pay for it."

"Ten bucks."

"I'll give you fifteen."

"You got a deal."

The car? I hoped you'd ask.

It was a 1932 Ford roadster, full fendered, a Model 18, which means the first year of the classic Flathead V-8.

Yup, if I'd parked it in my folks' back yard . . . except that on the other hand, it was the first and last time I ever sold a car for more than I paid for it, and the point here, if not the moral, is we were dealing with and learning with cars no one else wanted, the very definition of supply and demand.

I knew from the magazines and my own sense of aesthetics what I wanted my car to look like and be. The neighboring big city was a port and had junk-yards heaped with raw material.

There was the day I poked and pawed and came up with a radiator and grille for a '32 Ford, already the classic look in my crowd.

I lugged the assembly to the yard office. "How much?"

"Five bucks."

"OK, here," I said as I fished in my pocket.

"You're buying? I thought you were selling. Twenty-five bucks."

And that's how they stayed in business.

Not that I cared, because I was so happy to find that grille that I all but danced all the way home, and that night at dinner it was all I could think of.

Mom and Dad were happy for me, while not having any idea why it mattered so much, but then later, when I'd bought an MG-TC my dad wondered why I hadn't picked a Willys Jeepster. Looked just as funny and old, to him, while with the Jeepster I'd have room for my friends.

(I explained, as delicately as I could, that I only wanted room for one, count her, one, friend in my car.)

As I gained confidence, I drove farther from home and began worrying about minor points of the vehicle code, like not having fenders, a lack that also bothered passengers in the rain.

Almost as good as the wrecking yards then were the mail-order catalogs. Sure, there were joke items and outright frauds. But they also offered stuff we needed, such as cycle fenders complete with brackets.

Soon as the box arrived I called Skip, who had a welding torch, also mail order, and while he didn't have any proper welding rod, his mom had plenty of coat hangers and any metal was good enough for us.

So I plunked the box of fenders into the rumbleseat—which was a trunk with a seat (kids, ask granddad)—and off I went.

One more time there I was, driving north on the Merritt Parkway, one of the world's pioneer limited-access highways, scenic and landscaped and the jewel of Connecticut's highway department, when my rearview mirror was full of red lights.

The trooper was brisk and courteous.

I handed over license and registration, he ran the check and wondered, where were my fenders?

In the rumbleseat, I said, and I showed him the equipment and explained that at that very moment I was on my way to have the brackets welded on, so I could attach the fenders.

OK, he said, and I drove away, confidence intact.

My friend Skip welded the brackets, we bolted on the fenders, and I headed home.

Couple miles down the road, the brackets came loose and the fenders fell off. No harm done, I collected the parts, stowed them, and drove on.

First thing next morning I headed north on the Merritt Parkway again and as you will have guessed, the same trooper stopped me and wondered what the Sam Hill I was up to this time.

I showed him the broken welds and the brackets and fenders and assured him I was on my way to redo the job.

Move it, he barked, and I did.

Skip fired up the torch and fed the coat hangers to the flame, and again no prize for guessing, I headed home, the fenders fell off, I went back the next morning and there he was—and it just this minute struck me, he might have been waiting for me.

Here we are at those threatening words.

He pointed to the exit not far up the road and told me he was gonna sit there and watch me exit the parkway, and if he ever saw this pile of junk there again he'd throw the book at me, it would be a fast pitch and a heavy book, and I'd be really sorry. I nodded glumly and followed instructions.

But wait! Things get better.

It's my notion that somehow before I was born I was given the choice between being smart or being lucky, and I was just smart enough to pick lucky.

As in, nostalgia was about to be born, and an older guy who wanted to restore a Model A made me an offer. It was more than I'd paid, $125 comes to mind now, and much less than I'd spent, but what mattered more was I had my eye on another car. The official papers said it was a 1935 Ford roadster but folklore held that you could remove the homely '35 grille and front fenders and hood and replace them with the more shapely parts from a 1936, and such proved to be the case.

Beautiful car, one of the nicest designs that ill-fated genius Edsel Ford ever did. Mine was in black, with red-and-white checkerboarding on the vents in the hood sides. It had a top and side curtains that deflected the rain, and the girl who'd missed the Junior Prom 'cause I hadn't known that Ford fuel pump pushrods wear out, forgave me and I got to use the ol' armstrong heater—ask yer dad.

We'll skip the '32 roadster and the '37 two-door and the arrival of sports cars and my realization that no matter what I did to an old Ford, it would still be an old Ford.

Here we are in the here-and-now and I'm driving my farm truck and I pass an *American Graffiti* replica, a yellow '32 Ford coupe with independent suspension front and rear, flawless paint on the fiberglass body, automatic transmission, disc brakes, air conditioning, big-block V-8.

Can't help thinking, there's discretionary income going to a good cause, bet he's pored over the catalogs and had the best professional help and never mutters good-luck mantras when he turns the key.

Despite all that I can't but wonder, in the transition from fumbling with junk to assembling works of art, was something lost?

Does ordering a perfect replica body equal rummaging through the piles of debris and finding that 1932 grille?

I don't think so.

HOT ROD DREAMS: Youngsters—and oldsters—dream big in their small hot rod pedal cars, soapbox derby racers, and King Midget cars.

The WAY It WAS

By Albert Drake

Albert Drake built his first hot rod—a '29 A-V8 Ford roadster—in 1951. Since then, he has built and driven dozens of rods.

Albert is also one of the most prolific of hot-rodding journalists. More than 300 of his articles have appeared in a magazines including *Street Rodder, Street Rod Action, Rodder's Digest, Popular Cars, Hot Rod Mechanix, Street Rodding Illustrated, Street Rods Unlimited, Custom Car, Hot Rod and Custom,* and others. For the past sixteen years, he has written a monthly column for *Rod Action* entitled "'Fifties Flashback."

Albert was one of the first to wax nostalgic on hot rodding in his book *Hot Rodder!* This was followed by other memoirs and histories, including *Street Was Fun in '51, A 1950s Rod & Custom Builder's Dream Book, Herding Goats, Flat Out, The Big "Little GTO" Book,* and a hot-rodding novel, *Beyond the Pavement.*

This essay looks back at the early days of hot rodding in all their glory.

THE WAY IT WAS: Or at least the way we wish it was. Larry Watson, well-known painter and customizer, leans out the window of his first custom car in the late 1950s, the '51 Chevy known as Grape Vine.

The first hot rod I remember seeing was in 1947, along Harbor Drive in my hometown of Portland, Oregon. We had stopped to make a left turn, and a roadster coming the other way made a right turn and shot up the street ahead of us. I was just getting interested in cars, and I asked my father what kind of car it was. "All kinds," he said, as the low-slung car sped off, and he explained that the two boys had built it themselves. I was impressed, and watched as it blasted off into the distance.

It was 1951 before I became seriously interested in such cars. By then, a revolution had occurred in automotive styling and customizing. Every Detroit automobile had outgrown the prewar body shapes and the new cars were longer, lower, sleeker. Therefore, many people wanted to make their older car look more modern—or at least more stylish.

Today we look back at pre-1949 cars with a wistful eye, but at the time they seemed drab—high and boxy with plain interiors, and painted just a handful of standard boring colors, such as black, dark blue, or gray. The owners of older cars wanted to update them, whereas the owners of new cars wanted to individualize them.

By 1950, the hobby of building, customizing, and rejuvenating cars had hit like a thunderclap, and the streets were full of neat cars, from Los Angeles to Portland and spreading across the country. It didn't take much to make old and new cars more exciting. In alley garages and backstreet workshops, people were using lowering blocks or shackles, fender skirts, dual exhausts with chrome "echo cans," deluxe seat covers, and a metallic paint job that made the guy next to you at the stoplight sit up and take notice. An aftermarket accessory business sprang up to provide the bolt-on items backyard builders needed—fender skirts, dual exhaust setups, lowering blocks for almost any car, bull-nose strips for '36 and '49-'50 Fords, full-disc hubcaps, chrome dash knobs, solid side panels for '28-'36 Fords, spotlights, metal sections to "blank out" the center grille of a '41 Ford (a modification that cut down on the car's cooling ability but it looked wild), and Continental kits.

Those '32-'36 Fords were abundant, inexpensive, looked good in stock condition, and—most people agreed—looked even better fixed up. A '36 Ford could be had for under $75. Shackles, solid side panels, dual exhausts, and white sidewall tires might cost another $50, and the result was a good-looking car. For a few bucks more, the spare-tire bracket could be cut so the tire rode close to the deck, and dual spotlights added. If the owner were lucky to find a pair of '37 DeSoto bumpers, he'd be traveling in style. If you had the desire to get your hands dirty, you could convert the mechanical brakes to hydraulic brakes, install a column shift, and perhaps a '40 Ford steering wheel (to indicate where the brakes had come from).

If you had a post-'38 car and a few bucks, you could have a body shop "nose and deck" it. They removed the hood and trunk ornaments, brazed in the holes, and installed an inside latch assembly so that the trunk, like the hood, could be opened from the inside. Some owners never got around to installing the trunk latch, and the lid would fly up and down at every bump until the lead fell out of the holes.

By 1950 in Portland, there were literally hundreds of cars that had been given the treatment. You spotted a fixed-up car every block—a lowered and skirted Chevy fastback, a '40 Ford with '49 Plymouth bumpers, a Nash Lafayette with dual pipes, a '39 Dodge coupe with inset license plate and painted a new Ford Crestliner color, chartreuse. Some had warmed-up engines, but most were stockers, and provided sharp everyday transportation.

There was an abundance of material to work with. People generally kept their cars during the war years when new-automobile production ceased—and folk generally kept their cars eight to ten years anyway in those days. The Oregon climate is fairly kind to metal, and there seemed to be an unlimited supply of working material. You'd see Model T's and A's being used as daily drivers, and for every old car on the road there seemed to be a dozen in driveways, fields, barns, and garages. The shortage of cars during and after World War II meant that a used car could command a solid price. By 1950, the supply was catching up with demand and prices quickly began to fall. A complete Model A could be had for as little as $5 to $20, although the average price was around $75.

When the Korean War broke out, good cars could be got for a song from draftees about to board a ship for Japan. A nice rod or custom cost from $100 to $500, and sometimes you could get one for nothing. My buddy Joe Tarkington got a fine maroon '36 Ford Phaeton when his brother was drafted. How I coveted that car! I would spend hours looking through the plexiglass side curtains at the chrome dash, column shift, the curve of the heavy body support behind the front seat, and the fine leather upholstery. I'd imagine what I could do, what friends I could win, if only I owned a car like that!

The '32-'36 Ford roadsters and Phaetons were always rare—in fact, there must be more around now than there were then, due in large part to aftermarket bodies. The '35-'36 Ford Phaeton was the ultimate car, with lovely curves and a body that longed for attention. The two most exquisite examples of the marque in my town were Mid Barbour and Wayne Mahaffey's two '35 Phaetons, and Eddie Duhon's '39 Ford four-door convertible. All three vehicles were black, with white chopped and padded tops. They had the idealized shape of the cars that I drew in my school notebooks.

Hot rods were everywhere, almost as if they were being turned out somewhere by factories of backyard mechanics. I was interested in any car that had been subjected to even slight modifications. I walked around the city feeling the thrill of anticipation as I looked up driveways, peered into garages, and scanned backyards. If I saw a Model A with 16-inch wheels parked at the curb, I shoved my face against the louvers in the side panels to see if I could make out the shadowy configuration of a V8, or twin carbs on a four-barrel. I dropped to my knees before the front bumper as if in worship of this machine to see whether the car had hydraulic brakes. Everything was new to me, and I savored the excitement of recognition when I could identify any alterations. I loved the smell of leather and oil-blowby in the cockpit, the curve of a '32 grille shell, and the shape of a Stromberg carburetor. I sought out these configurations until I truly believed that, at one time, I knew, at least by sight, every hot rod in Portland.

It's harder to generalize about the typical hot rod because they lent themselves to the handiwork of American ingenuity. They ran the gamut from nearly stock to highly modified track roadsters driven on the street. If there was a trend, it was to make the car lower, and this usually meant channeling the body. And then, there went the fenders! By law you had to have something over the tires, so you bobbed the rear fenders and built cycle fenders for the front. This was done by cutting a spare-tire cover into two halves, one for each front wheel, and fabricating brackets that would bolt to the backing plates. A 16-inch cover would fit over 16-inch tires but the radius wasn't uniform. The best covers came from old Cadillacs and Lincolns, which used

HOT ROD SCRAP-BOOK: Author Albert Drake's first cars, circa 1952–1953. Clockwise from top left: Albert in his nosed and decked '53 Merc. His custom '35 Ford with '37 Ford sheet metal and full-race Merc engine. A work-in-progress '33 Ford Tudor. His nosed and decked '37 Ford coupe, purchased for a mere $45. (Albert Drake collection)

larger tires. In spite of Oregon's annual 300 days of rain, there were an awful lot of cars with bobbed fenders.

How plentiful the raw material was! I can recall at least five '32 Ford coupes owned by friends that were bought in stock condition and then channeled almost immediately. A cutting torch took care of the floor and firewall, and some strap iron was worked into brackets for the body. Of course, if you got the body a little crooked, the doors wouldn't shut. If they did shut, they'd pop open when the body flexed—which it was doing constantly without a floorpan to keep it rigid. But what excitement as a

stocker, after a couple of hours with the torch, took on the appearance of a real California hot rod.

I remember my friend Gary's first '32. It was a green three-window that was used by a druggist for daily transportation and it was as stock as could be. Gary bought it, drove it for a few days, then took off the fenders and bumpers. We thought it looked sharp like that—especially after he'd put dual exhausts on the '32 engine. Gary decided that it sat too high, though. Over a weekend, he channeled the body several inches, mounted the grille and radiator ahead of the front crossmember, and built a longer hood. As that car came down the street Monday morning, we thought it was the meanest-looking rig imaginable. To get the rear tires to clear the body, Gary had punched out the wheel lugs and put in longer ones, then had put the wheels on backwards, which was a cheap and dirty, but highly imaginative, version of reversed rims. It's lucky the lug bolts didn't break under stress, but that was hot rodding in those days.

Gary drove his '32 like that for a couple weeks, and then channeled it again. The body must have been lowered over the frame about 12 inches, but because the frame wasn't lowered there was little room inside. You sat on a thin pad and hoped that your head didn't hit the roof at a sharp bump as Gary rumbled past those poor slobs who had to walk, or worse, take the bus. One *experienced* the engine—there were no floorboards or firewall, so all the fumes came back into the car. But there are few thrills in life like the one of climbing into a channeled '32 coupe after a dull day at high school, snuggling down among the crossmembers and exhaust pipes, and seeing the naked machinery at your feet and the ground a few inches beyond. I can still remember the sound of that engine. The distinctive grinding of the starter and then the noise of the ragged, choppy V8, the short shift lever, and the sometimes comforting, sometimes claustrophobic feel of the coupe's tiny cockpit.

Gary sold that coupe after a few months. Three years later he built another super-low coupe, a five-window, and this time he did it right. But what the hell, Deuces were plentiful.

Looking back, I'm amazed at the general impulse—mass hysteria, some might say—that compelled people to remove whatever was removable on a car and then cut away the body supports to make it as low as possible. Of course, whatever was removed was discarded—imagine the piles of stock fenders, bumpers, and hoods! The law—and parents—were totally opposed to the removal of such sundries as fenders, and I'm sure that everyone was warned. But to strip a car down seemed somehow natural; it was the first step toward creating a machine that resembled the examples we'd seen in magazines.

It also cost little or nothing to remove what was removable—it was certainly less expensive than buying and adding things to a car. Off with the stock air cleaner. Off with the fan assembly (everyone said they robbed the engine of horsepower). Off with whatever seemed superfluous or resembled the conventional—trunk handle, hood ornament, running boards, muffler, hood. One saw many cars with the hood removed and a chrome air cleaner topping an otherwise stock engine, the driver revving up a cloud of blue smoke at the stoplight.

There was something contagious about all this activity. A fixed-up car stood out against the grayness of ordinary traffic, and as you drove down Main Street and saw a '48 Ford convertible rumbling along with skirts, duals, nosed and decked, the Hollywood hubcaps spinning in the sun, you experienced that deep yearning—gotta have it!

Although one always felt limited by a lack of money, the act of driving was ridiculously unfettered. If you bought a $20 car, you could drive it off. If the plates on the car were current, they were valid; there was no transfer requirement. It was a good idea to have a driver's license, but hardly anyone bothered to get the title changed to his or her name, and few people I knew had liability insurance—or *any* kind of insurance, period.

Because it was so easy to drive anything, there were plenty of unsafe cars on the road with worn-out front ends, burned-out lights, or thin tires. Most cars of the '30s had mechanical brakes with worn clevises and pins—and even worse were the "cabledraulic" brakes of '37-'38 Fords, with rusty or stretched cables. I later had a '37 Ford coupe and to stop it I'd stand on the brake pedal, pulling up on the steering wheel for leverage—all without noticeable results.

Of course, we didn't want cars like those, with all their defective equipment. The cars we had seen in magazines, and a few we had seen on the streets of Portland, had shown us the ideal. Sleek, flawless metal, all chassis parts cleaned and painted or chrome plated, and a spotless interior. This was the ideal we all pursued, but the result generally fell far short of the mark. It's hard to be show-car perfect. A car without fenders will throw mud and water across the side of the body. Oil and gas will leak over an engine and on the firewall. Muddy feet will soon track up the carpet.

But the flaws were inherent in the process of building the car. Few cars in those days were disassembled and rebuilt; most were built piecemeal over a period of months, and many were never "finished."

HOT ROD HEAVEN: Photo-montage artist Peter Tytla creates fantastical images of car enthusiasts and their world, such as this illustration titled *Advanced Decay*. As Tytla writes: "This rare and advanced rust pile is the pride of Eric the Bone Man. He's from the old school, and if he likes you, after a lengthy conversation, he will let you go out to the yard, wander around, and even let you take tools so you can get parts for your hot rod. It's quite a trip down at Eric's as there's always a new discovery—but you have to watch out for those snakes." (Artwork © Peter Tytla)

BACKYARD RODS:
The Shifters Car Club creates their rods as a group, working together to get their rides ready. This is backyard stuff, just like the old days; no one has a fancy workshop, but most everyone is handy at wrenching and creative engineering. These rods are a slice of what the members drive, all of them just way cool in a world of candy-coated billet rods. Jeff Vodden owns the chopped '30 Model A; Alex Idzardi the '29 Model A roadster pickup; Anthony Castaneda the '31 Model A; and Kevin Sledge the '24 Model T roadster. Kevin's roadster is an intriguing mix of hot rod parts finished with a wonderfully applied patina. Built tight with a stubby body on a 98-inch wheelbase, the roadster uses only the basics for its underpinnings with an owner-built round-tube frame, suicide front end with dropped axle, T-rear spring, and drum brakes on the rear only. Kevin added what he calls the "Pep Boys Rattle Can Red" cowl panel that sweeps back into scallops, highlighted with white pinstriping. Powering the roadster is a 331 '49 Cadillac with '59 Caddy heads, a Howard cam, a four-pot Cragar aluminum manifold topped with 8BA Ford carburetors, and homemade headers. The interior features a wood dash, Stewart Warner gauges, red-and-black vinyl bench seat, a Covelo Metalflake steering wheel, and a chromed horn button spinner. (Photograph © David Fetherston)

Most hot rods had unpainted chassis, or only the visible parts were painted. There were rough edges, the places where parts from two different cars refused to merge. There were holes in the firewall, oodles of old wires hung from the dash; there were rough welds, lousy workmanship, bad ideas, botched hopes, and aborted plans. We desired perfection, but had to settle for the humanly imperfect.

Some cars were clearly illegal—they lacked fenders, horn, windshield wiper, or some essential equipment. Some cars were clearly dangerous—they were worn out or badly built. They had too much go but too little whoa. Some of the weird engine swaps clearly taxed the builder's ingenuity. In place of motor mounts one fellow had his engine resting on a piece of two-by-four board jammed between the frame rails! I recall another Flathead V8 in a Model A coupe where the builder split the wishbones and wired them to the frame. Whoever put the V8 in my roadster moved the steering box from an Oldsmobile almost to the ground, where it hit every curb or bump, in addition to placing the drag link at a severe angle. There were always little things you somehow never got around to doing. For months I drove without a headlight switch, and turned the lights on by twisting two wires together under the car. The headlights were mounted on the frame horns, and people kept backing into them, knocking them out of adjustment. Headlights were a problem anyway; you could always tell a fenderless car at night because the headlights shook so badly. And there were bald tires, leaky gas tanks, rusty water from the radiator—all this as opposed to the "typical" beautiful rod of today.

But it's important to realize that these cars were used for daily transportation. No one I knew

GETTING AROUND

The Beach Boys sang "I Get Around," and the same applies to this slick Lemon Chrome Yellow '31 Ford coupe. Builder Dave Tarvin figured if he was going to get around, he wanted to do it in an early-style rod emulating what a guy would have built in 1958. Most Model As are usually chopped but not channeled, or vice versa. Dave did both—a 4-inch channel and 3-inch chop. Tim Kennedy at Jimmy's Rod Shop shot the paint. Dave did a custom frame with a dropped and drilled axle, Posie Super Slide spring with '48 Ford spindles, '41 Ford brakes, and '55 Buick finned drums. Power comes from a 355-cubic inch Chevy with TRW 10:1 pistons topped by an Offenhauser tri-pack manifold and three Rochester two-barrel carbs. Keeping the 106-inch wheelbase rolling are a set of ruby red solid 15-inch Ford wheels with Baldy hubcaps and chrome beauty rings. These are capped with whitewalled Firestone bias-ply tires, really setting the yellow rod off right on its all-chrome suspension. Other nostalgic touches include the '41 Ford cab-over pickup headlights, '48 Chevy taillights, and 10-gallon Moon tank. It's one ultra-cool nostalgia rod, built with an appreciation of classic hot rodding. (Photograph © David Fetherston)

kept a car in the garage to be taken out only for car shows or an occasional drive. These hot rods were driven everywhere, in all kinds of weather. They were parked in places where they were subjected to bad drivers, rain, and vandalism. One had to accept the imperfections of chipped paint, small dents, and worn upholstery.

I remember seeing a guy with a '34 Ford five-window near my house. He was young, married, and already a father. The coupe was apparently his only transportation, and each week you'd see it in a different stage of completion. He must have decided that he was going to hammer the lid down, because one day he drove past with the entire roof cut off; a few days later he came by with the chopped top tack-welded in place. He didn't have the glass cut yet, not even the windshield; it was raining, and he had his family with him. It took him a month to get the job done, but he drove it every day in between. Talk about devotion.

My Old HOT ROD

By Jay Carnine

Jay Carnine grew up in California in the mid-1950s, and like many of his friends, hot rods and all they stood for became the focus of his life. He watched goggle-eyed as the first hot rod he ever saw rolled down the street. Soon after, he built his own machine and was competing on the dry lakes and dragstrips. He fabricated performance parts in high-school shop class, cruised Main Street, and busted his knuckles wrenching on rods in his family's garage.

Neither Jay nor his buddies ever became famous hot rodders or racers, though; they were just your typical American boys living the hot rodder's life.

This essay recounts Jay's memories of drive-ins, damsels, and drag racing.

YOUNG RODDERS: In this 1960 painting, "Big" Ron is strapped for cash to run his rod.

Hot rodding for me started about age eight when my dad and uncle took me to one of Los Angeles' first hot rod shows. There were more than a few new cars there, but what impressed me the most were a couple of roadsters on display. The roadsters were what I thought a car should be. They were probably too loud, too fast, and entirely too much fun, but to my unsophisticated mind, better than any other car I'd ever seen.

Prior to this time I'd been around what were probably some more than interesting coupes and sedans owned by a couple of dads' hot rodding friends, but other than realizing they went down the road a little stronger than most cars, I wasn't impressed too much. The roadsters though, they struck me with something that's stayed with me all of my life.

Even so, at eight years old I knew I had a ways to go before I could get involved with hot rods and even farther to go before I could get involved with roadsters. Not to mention it would be close to eight years before I got my driver's license.

From reading the *Motor Trend* magazines passed on by my granddad, I had a pretty good idea of what I wanted. The tough part was getting to the point where I could actually drive a car—never mind that buying one was completely beyond me at that point.

I didn't forget, though, and after a few years passed, I found myself paying more attention to hot rods and customs running the streets, and now that I was paying attention, it was surprising to find there were more of them than I'd realized.

Once my friends and I got into junior high school we started noticing modified cars more than ever. One of the most interesting cars was a customized '50 Ford coupe right down the street. The coupe's simple modifications set it apart from most other cars: nosed and decked, a set of pipes with outlets molded into the bottom part of the bumper guards, skirts lowered just a couple of inches, and an interior filled with white tuck-and-roll upholstery. The coupe was painted a creamy white. The engine ran a pair of carburetors, a set of aluminum heads, and that was about it. It made for a good running stand-out car and made me wonder why dad didn't do something similar to his just about perfect, two-year-old black '50 Ford sedan. The simple answer was, the owner of the '50 Ford coupe was single, had a good job, and at twenty-two, he had the extra money to do things like that. Dad had a good job in the oil fields and worked hard, but what extra money there was went to the family budget. No surprise there for anyone who's ever had a family.

Once we rolled into high school, it seemed like there were more and more hot rods running the streets. To our unfettered minds it didn't take much to qualify a car in the hot rod category. A dual exhaust system—commonly called "pipes"—was a start, and for some a nice set of wheel covers or hubcaps, maybe a touch of lowering, and that was it. Car finished.

That was enough for most guys, but for some of us, it was the hot rod engines we lusted after. There was something primal, almost evil in the way they sounded. We weren't alone in our thinking either. We saw more than a few adults cast a wary eye toward these mechanical beasts. Something happened when hot rods with serious, strong-running engines rolled by on the streets, or better yet when they idled into a parking lot. They commanded attention, but what they really demanded was caution. The kind of caution you'd use if a big jungle cat stepped into the scene and was deciding on who was for lunch.

Somewhere in here we discovered girls. Along with this discovery came to the realization we needed a car, any car if we were going to court these beautiful young women. We didn't know we were courting them and in fact didn't know that we'd jumped headlong into the gene pool, but jumped we had and like all the rest, were swimming blindly along.

There weren't too many serious relationships with young women in junior high school. Perhaps our choice, but more than likely their choice. Once we entered high school, it was a whole other world. With no one in the gang owning a car and not a one of us possessing a driver's license, we didn't stand a chance. No big deal, we decided. We figured we'd get a license, then maybe a car, and we'd be in Fat City as far as dating these young women went. And like you'd think, we weren't fooling anyone but ourselves.

Time slid by and we finally got to the point where we were just short of getting the fabled learner's permit, never mind the driver's license. We felt like our lives were going somewhere or at the least were about to change. Maybe they were. It seemed like things started happening and somewhere in there, the folks got to the point where they had no problems with turning us loose on the world.

It didn't matter that we were on foot. We had absolutely no problem walking the two miles or so to the Fosters Freeze malt shop and hamburger joint. With a midnight curfew, there was plenty of time to see what we could see. What we saw was that Fosters Freeze was one of the best places there was to see hot rods and customs. Many of the cars we saw were common to the time, but today it would be a special treat to see any one of them.

Two of our favorite cars were a GMC-powered '41 Chevy coupe and a Flathead-powered '47 Ford business coupe. Both cars ran sans hood, but what

initially attracted us was spotting the small group of older guys standing around, drinking cokes and malts, talking easily, and watching carefully whenever a handful of nobodies like us approached their cars. They didn't have to worry about us, though; we knew what the unwritten rules were as far as looking a guy's car over.

Once the older guys—older being seventeen to twenty-one—figured we knew what we were doing, they went back to what they were doing while we looked the cars over and listened to what we could of the conversation. As long as we kept our mouths shut or at the least didn't ask any really stupid questions, no one seemed to mind if we hung around and took part. For us, it was an education beyond compare. These were guys who'd built cars, driven cars, and even raced cars. Seemed too, the most knowledgeable guys were the ones who didn't talk much. Their cars did all the talking for them. Just standing around listening, we found there was a tremendous amount of information being swapped back and forth. Most of it, we didn't have a clue what it meant, but every one of us, for days afterward, could recite just about word-for-word what was said.

Hot rods turned into an all-consuming thing with me. With my fairly large collection of dog-eared *Hot Rod Magazines* as well as a few of the small-sized *Rod & Custom* and *Car Craft* magazines to refer to, it didn't take long to learn what Isky Cams, Offenhauser heads, ⅜ x ⅜ Flatheads, and four-carbed GMC engines were all about.

I think we drove Dad's hot rod-owning friends crazy with questions at times. They had some interesting stories, but the very best for me was listening to Dad's modest but interesting tales about the cars he grew up with and the times he went to Rogers Dry Lake to try out his friend's latest car or engine modification.

Running the dry lakes in Dad's era was fairly primitive stuff. Camping on the lakes could be a tough go at times, but the race cars were usually driven to the lakes, unloaded, run, and if nothing broke, they were loaded back up and driven home. He knew a few guys who towed their race car to the lakes and once in a while they passed them grinding away on the long and winding grades up the highway toward the desert and its dry lakes. At times, the tow vehicle with race car tagging along behind

would pass them. Tow bar still hooked up to the tow car or pickup, somebody in the race-car driver's seat and the race-car engine running in an effort to help the heavily loaded rig over the hill. Towing the long desert grades in the summer, even at night, was a test for any car, let alone one loaded to the gills.

California's cool and comfortable winters would have been the perfect time to run the dry lakes, but once the rains came, the lakes flooded and that was it for the season. When World War II started, the government took over Rogers Dry Lake and it became a test area for top-secret work on America's aircraft. It didn't really matter; racing was on hold for the duration and most of the guys who'd been involved were in the service.

I never tired of hearing Dad's dry-lakes stories. From a simpler time, to be sure, but the hard work and technical knowledge required is the same now

as it was then. Do it wrong and you'd be dragging home a bunch of broken parts.

Time flies, they say, but for a guy desiring a driver's license, it seemed to crawl. Eventually, enough time slid by for me to be up for a driver's license. I'd studied so hard and really paid attention in driver's training class that the written and then the driving test turned out to be fairly easy. I thought I'd lost some points when I locked up the brakes for an errant driver blowing a stop sign, but either the license examiner was the bravest guy in the world or he'd seen it all. He didn't say a word. After all that, the only thing I got gigged for was the not-too-swift parallel parking I'd done. It didn't make any difference, I wasn't planning on parking very much anyway.

About four months after I got my license I got a good job in an auto parts store that paid good money

and Dad sold me his most cherry black '50 Ford sedan. A couple of weeks after that I had a set of duals on it and was on my way to owning a genuine hot rod. Somewhere in here, the car was lowered in front, a set of the seldom seen small '56 Chevy hubcaps were installed, and the little '50 was looking pretty good. Sounded good too. The pipes running a pair of medium-length glasspacks had the sweetest sound I ever heard on a car. Maybe it was the time and maybe it was the perspective, and more than likely it was

because it was my car and the summer I had it was especially sweet. There's something about having a driver's license, a few bucks in your pocket, and owning your own car that makes life free and easy.

Like you'd think, the freedom would have been curtailed a bit if I didn't stay on the straight and narrow. The sweetness was still there and sometimes it was made even sweeter by the late-night street racing we got involved with. At first, none of this involved going out in the country to a deserted road and doing it with a relative degree of safety. If you found yourself at a red light with what you felt was an evenly matched car, once the green popped, the race was on. Most of the races were nothing more than a quick launch, a low-gear run across the intersection, tires screaming a bit, pipes roaring, and a chunk of second-gear rubber tossed off when you did a good if not great speedshift, approaching 50 mph or so and letting off the gas. With the cars we drove at the time and considering the horsepower available, a short race with not too much speed on was enough to determine who really did have the fastest car.

What we learned from all this was two basic things. Mainly that the other car wasn't always what it seemed, and the second thing, stupidity. The stupidity, sad to say, was ours. Having a race from an in-town stoplight wasn't the smartest thing we ever did. Half the time you'd get caught, get a ticket, lose your license for a week, two weeks, a month and worse. Not to mention being grounded by Dad, which meant you couldn't go anywhere for a while.

The part about the other cars not being what they seemed was our surprise introduction to sleepers. Sleepers being cars that looked stock or close to it and most times they had a serious engine that didn't sound serious, but they'd still clean your clock. To top if off there were more than a few good-looking '50 Oldsmobile coupes and two-door sedans running the streets, and they would kill you with their hard, strong launch across the street. The hard launch made possible by the very low-geared low gear in the four-speed hydramatic transmission. Not to mention their rear suspension seemed to plant the tires against the pavement pretty good. Later on when we were running stronger flatheads, although not too strong, the Oldsmobiles would still kill us because we would be spinning the tires on our coupes while the Oldsmobiles simply drove across the intersection and away. We were quick learners though. After a few of those we learned to avoid the Oldsmobiles.

We paid attention as well when some of the Oldsmobiles started showing up with built engines. It didn't seem to matter whether they had the much-lusted-after and famed Cad-Lasalle '37 floor-shift transmission with tall shift stick topped by the ever popular eight-ball or the four-speed Hydro. They were cars our Fords couldn't touch.

About this time, we got serious about our Ford coupes. Coupes because most everybody in the gang owned one, and I'd found a cherry '50 Ford coupe right down the street, bought it, pulled all the good stuff out of the absolutely cherry '50 Ford sedan, and took the sedan to the junkyard. Yeah, I was stupid. And yeah, I still regret it.

After I'd owned the coupe for a while I got hold of a 303 Olds engine, Hydro and all. I did a fairly nice swap, considering I didn't own anything remotely resembling a welder. Motor mounts were from CT automotive as was the dropped tie rod. A starter changeover to move the starter from the stock Olds position on the left, where it interfered with the Ford steering box, over to the right. A '48 Cadillac starter so the solenoid wouldn't conflict with the tie rod, a home-built exhaust system welded up by a friend who used a rented gas welder and coat hanger wire for rod. Sounds strange, but it worked fine. In the end, I had a good-running little car that would fry the tires on command, but it really wasn't too fast.

My friends and I did the black primer bit. Most of the paint jobs on our '49-'50 Ford coupes were faded factory colors with a few primer spots from nosing, decking, and getting the dents out. Primer was easy and cheap to apply at home. Mine ended up more than interesting first time around as, not knowing any better, I shot it with black lacquer primer and used the 100 psi straight from the compressor to the spray gun. Who knew about regulators, let alone moisture traps in those days? The paint was probably half dry when it hit the body surface and ended up looking as though a giant sheet of 80-grit wet/dry sandpaper had been glued on. Felt just about as smooth too. A weekend of sanding for four of us and shooting it again with the proper spray equipment left it a nice suede finish.

The tough part about painting at home was simply getting access to an air compressor. With Dad working in the oil patch, he could usually bring home a compressor for the day, said compressor belonging to one of the oilfield supply outfits. If not, there were rental outfits. With the group "spraygun"—which actually belonged to one of our dads—we were in business. At least we thought so.

A few guys shot primer and even painted their complete cars with a vacuum cleaner. Some vacuum cleaners came with a wide range of accessories and with a cheap spray gun plugged into the outlet end, you were in business. Sort of. Most of these paint jobs were pretty sad looking, partly due to lack of painting experience, partly due to a poor choice in paints, and partly due to the poor spraying qualities of a vacuum cleaner.

Enterprising guys primed bodywork with a fly sprayer. These were simple gadgets, not seen at all nowadays. They looked a bit like a tire pump with a screw-on metal can attached. You filled the can with purchased fly spray, shot it at the potential victims by pumping the handle, and hoped for the best. Most times all you got was a bad-smelling room with a poisonous cloud. Fly sprayers were cheap enough to buy, so guys loaded the can with primer, and shot the car. Some guys got pretty good with vacuum cleaners and fly sprayers, and at times, it was difficult to tell what kind of paint spray device was used.

Rattle cans were new at the time and didn't have the greatest paint in the world. One buddy painted his '50 Merc coupe a metallic green with rattle cans. It sounded like a good idea at the time, but like many of what we thought were good ideas, it didn't work in practice. He started with a dozen cans and ended up buying eight more. The big drag was getting all the cans well shaken. Even then, the paint ended up thin and uneven and the car didn't look all that great. In the end, he paid more for the rattle cans than he would have for "real" paint.

Black was the favored color for a completely primered car, although some sported red oxide or light gray. One '41 Chevy coupe nearby was done in all white primer. Somewhere along the line, some of the lowrider contingent discovered that white primer mixed with a bit of toner made a neat finish. For a while, there were quite a few pink and purple lowriders running around—a suede rainbow, for sure.

For the few that didn't care what color their car was, there was always the "mistake" paint. This was simply a gallon of enamel, or sometimes lacquer, that the paint-mix guy had screwed up; these were usually refused by paint shops, and for good reason. Typically, one of the toner colors was left out, or too much of one color added. Sometimes, it was painfully obvious when comparing the mixed paint with the color chip. These cans of paint were stored under the paint-mix bench and had a dollop of the color on the lid for identification. The stores usually sold them

out for two bits on the dollar. Quite a bargain, when you figure a gallon of red enamel cost about $10 at the time.

As far as the painted-versus-primered hot rods, a lot depended on where you lived. In my town, many cars were in just primer and ran that way for years. In almost all cases, though, primer was viewed as a step toward a finished paint job. Problem for most of us was the simple lack of money. We usually spent our money on engines, drivelines, and tires. The guys that didn't do the hot engine bit spent their money on paint and wheels. My town was somewhat poor, loaded with blue-collar oil patch and farm workers and all the related industries, which was one reason why a lot of rods ran in primer. The historic, touristy, and richer town to the north almost always had cars with a real paint job, and I don't remember seeing any rods from there running in solid primer.

Fun times for sure. Dangerous? Sometimes. Not so smart? Yeah, not so smart. Would I do it again? Not today, no way.

The past is past and life then wasn't so complex. At least about cars, girls, a whole other story. Which translated means the back roads really were pretty deserted and to an extent that made what we did reasonably safe. We weren't running the horrendous speeds that some of the modern-day street racers can run. Even so, it doesn't make it ok and it wouldn't have taken a very complex chain of circumstance to turn it into a tragedy. Which doesn't make it a moral story or anything along those lines. It just makes it a story from a quieter and a simpler time.

Sometimes I get to thinking and now and then I harken back to the days when me and the gang started driving. Aside from the freedom we'd gained, it meant we could date some of the desirable young women we met at school, the skating rink, Fosters Freeze, and other places. Dates for the most part that took place at the skating rink, movies, the beach, and most times ending up at Fosters Freeze.

The beach was quite a draw for us and it's surprising how much time we spent there. A little swimming, a lot of body surfing, but most of the time was spent hanging out with the girls, talking to them, actually listening when they talked to us and learning a little bit about them. As well as learning a little bit about ourselves.

Facing page,
CLASSIC HOT ROD ADVERTISEMENTS

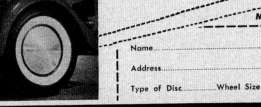

Hot Rods—How and Why!

The following essay was printed in a pamphlet published in the early 1960s by the Southern California Timing Association. It was designed to entice people to join the group in working toward safer racing and a better image for hot rods. As the SCTA stated, it was the "Sponsors of the World's Safest Automotive Speed Trials."

Nearly twenty-five years ago the first hot rod made its initial run on a dry lake bed in the Mohave desert under the official timing and safety standards of what was to become the oldest and most respected timing association for hot rodders in the world, the "Southern California Timing Association."

From that day to present is a story of faster speeds with greater safety.

After approximately 25,000 timed runs the accident rate is less than one tenth of 1 percent, a remarkable tribute to the fine technical inspection and rigid safety standards of S.C.T.A.

In the beginning 100 mph was a respected achievement. In 1961 on the El Mirage Lake bed near Palmdale, speeds in excess of 227 mph were recorded. However, even with the increased number of cars running each year and the much higher speeds, over the period of a quarter of a century, the accident rate has continued to decline. Too bad that our highways cannot boast of a similar record.

Hot rodding genius and hard work will continue to build faster, safer cars and S.C.T.A. will continue to keep them running safely.

Each month from May through October S.C.T.A. conducts speed trials for S.C.T.A. members and their guests at El Mirage dry lake, about a twenty-one hour drive from Los Angeles. Here our advance crew lays out a measured course 200 feet wide and 2½ miles long near the center of the smooth, hard lake bed. When this has been properly marked, J. Otto Crocker, our chief timer since the beginning, sets up his mile second clocks, which are recognized as the world's most accurate timing equipment and cars are timed through a measured ¼ mile near the center of the course. This allows no less than a mile deceleration area before turning off the course to return via the edge of the lake bed to the starting line.

Nearly sixty classes from the street driven "stocker" to the highly modified "tankers" are open to cars passing technical inspection and safety checks similar to those used at drag strips; however, only S.C.T.A. members may hold records.

After the first ten years of successful racing on the dry lakes, two forward thinking members named Wally Parks and Bob Petersen decided that the hot rodders were ready for bigger and better things. It is to their everlasting credit that S.C.T.A. presents Bonneville National Speed Trials each year about the third week in August at the Bonneville Salt Flats near Wendover, Utah.

The trials and tribulations of these two gentlemen and the rest of the S.C.T.A. Board would make pages of History in Hot Rodding. Suffice it to say that their efforts were rewarded by the world renowned and respected event, the greatest of them all, Bonneville Speed Week.

Following are a few of the names of those who through the years have come forth to do their part, some are still active—J. Otto Crocker, Bob Higbee, Tom Bryant, Jim Lindsley, Glen Deeds, Fred Willert, Bob Brisette, Emil Grisotti, Harry Woerner, Bill Graham, Ak Miller, Bill Burke, Multy Aldrich, Bill Davis, John Narry, Dean Batchelor, Paul Stratton, Jim Khougaz, Carroll Thompson, Bill Backman, John Bartlet, Roy Richter, Marvin Lee, Bozzy Willis. These and many more have and continue to bring forth the Miracle of Bonneville.

Although unpaid, they still come up from the ranks of S.C.T.A. to demonstrate their faith in American youth and the right to free enterprise.

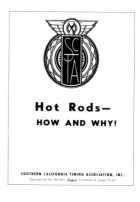

**Hot Rods—
HOW AND WHY!**

SOUTHERN CALIFORNIA TIMING ASSOCIATION, INC.
"Sponsors of the World's Safest Automotive Speed Trials"

Not long after we started driving, the beaches of Santa Barbara beckoned. We could not resist. Our perceptions were that Santa Barbara was a beautiful, but somewhat touristy and richer town. Perception or not, the Santa Barbara beaches were a small but exotic destination for us. The drive on the coastal highway was one of the best ones around and we ran it every chance we got.

The best part about running the coastal highway was when you got to the Rincon. The ocean was right up against the highway on one side and the railroad tracks were on the other. At the time, steam locomotives were common and sometimes we'd find ourselves headed south for home about the same time the Daylight Streamliner, California's premier passenger train, was headed south.

Seeing the Daylight was always a special treat. With it's brightly painted orange, black-and-silver-colored streamlined engine with passenger cars painted to match, it was a vivid spectacle when seen up against the green hills of early summer.

Not only seeing the Daylight, but hearing it as well entered into the experience. There was something in the song the steam engines sang that struck you to the very core of your being. After a couple of more than short years, the song was never again to be heard along the coast.

There was nothing quite like sailing down the coast in a '50 Ford sedan that sang its own song through the sweet-sounding pipes, listening to the soft beach winds flowing through the car, a beautiful young woman beside you, and best of all, racing the Daylight down the coast highway mile after mile. Not a word was said. It was enough to listen to the sounds from the powerful steam engine that was at times, less than a hundred feet away.

The Ford and the Daylight were a mix of sounds that were natural to the day and nothing that could ever be put together by the conductor of the best orchestra ever could make such music.

Every generation and every time has their own special things and I hope this little trip down memory lane has you leaning back in the chair, eyes closed, hearing the sounds of a sweet-running flathead spinning out its own song against the mighty resonance that came forth from the Daylight.

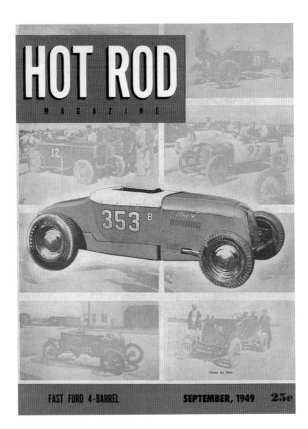

LEGENDS

In the beginning it had been a 1952 Chevrolet convertible, but as a result of his toil and sweat, plus every dime or dollar he could spare from the money he earned at odd jobs after school and on weekends, it was now an eye-catching combination of several car manufacturers' products.

Robert Sidney Bowen, *Hot Rod Angels*, 1960

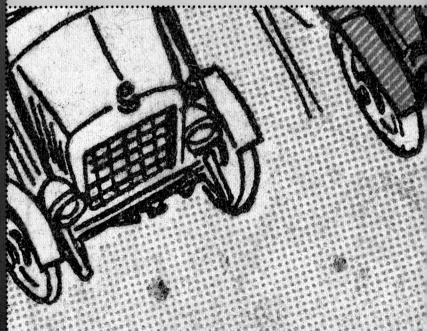

BACKROADS RACE: *American Graffiti* was George Lucas' memoir of his own teenage years in Modesto, California, shown in a series of anecdotes of one night's activities of four main characters who have graduated or are about to graduate from Dewey High School in the summer of '62. Screaming down Frates Road in this reenactment, the evil black '55 and the original chopped five-window head into hot rod history in one of the greatest film race scenes ever. (Photograph © David Fetherston)

ICONS

By David Fetherston

David Fetherston is a journalist and photographer who simply loves automobiles—and especially hot rods and customs. Classically trained in photography and filmmaking in Australia, for the past twenty years he's been living in California, where he writes and photographs for all the top hot rod and custom magazines; publishes books; produces videos; and runs an advertising agency specializing in high performance. He is the author of numerous books, including *Heroes of Hot Rodding*, *Great American Street Machines*, *Moon Equipped*, *Goodguys Hot Rod Chronicles*, and several histories of the Barris Kustoms.

David's not just a behind-the-scenes enthusiast, however. He has also raced motorcycles, rallied cars, built off-road racing cars, road raced with the Sports Car Club of America, and crewed on several land speed cars at the Bonneville Salt Flats.

In this historical essay, he looks back on the roots of hot rodding and custom cars.

In the rough and tumble backstreets of 1930s America, hot rodding was born kicking and screaming. Young men were thrilled by the mechanical and technological developments of a brave new world. They were gripped by Charles Lindbergh's flight across the Atlantic and awed by land speed racers Malcolm Campbell and Henry Seagrave besting 200 mph on Daytona Beach, and they listened with held breath, to an endless supply of news-breaking stories of daring, from events like the Indy 500. At their own local dirt speedways, many of these budding automotive buffs dreamed about their heroes as they got their thrills hanging on the fence, breathing in the smell of oil and fumes of race cars, and getting dirt thrown in their faces. The need for speed could be satisfied by the allure of these crazy new automobiles.

California was hot rodding's birthplace. A dramatic societal change was taking place in the American Midwest and South as people were being forced off their land by drought and poverty when the Great Depression took hold. People began desperately looking for other avenues of work and other locations to settle, with fresh opportunities. California seemed the promised land of milk and honey, luring many people westward. A new life was beginning: small businesses developed, women joined the workforce, and families grew. The children of these determined and courageous folks became the parents of the grassroots hot rod movement. Dean Moon came to California with his parents from Minnesota in the

early 1930s, Vic Edelbrock arrived from Kansas, and Bill Devin and Wally Parks all originated in Oklahoma. And waiting for them were native sons of California, youths like Ed Winfield, Ed Iskenderian, and Andy Brizio.

By the beginning of the 1930s, the first full generation of production automobiles had evolved from the Model T Ford. With more than 15 million sold, there were many Model Ts awaiting a buyer for just a few dollars. Kids could piece together a working Model T with creativity and a little spare cash. And with some ingenuity, they could "hot up" their steed. These kids made up the majority of the early speed freaks. They hung out at the speedways and listened to the races on the newfangled radio, and they took the speedway's performance parts to the street. They had seen Ed Winfield racing and knew about his "secret" parts. They figured it all out quickly: with these parts, they could put more horsepower to the pavement than Henry Ford ever imagined his Tin Lizzy would stand.

If necessity is the mother of invention, then Ed Winfield was an obedient son. His years working as a teenage apprentice for famed race-car builder Harry Miller gave him a clear vision of power. Winfield moved from shop kid to riding mechanic by age fifteen and driver at twenty-one.

At Miller's shop, Ed was instructed in the latest performance developments, learning the black arts of engine building, carburetor design, and tuning.

Left, **RAT:** One of the first throwback, fifties-style rat rods was this '32 Ford roadster owned by Robert Kitilla. Propulsion came courtesy of a Hemi Chrysler fed by six Stromberg 97 carburetors topped by baloney-slicer air stacks. Bill Ganahl was at the wheel here at El Mirage dry lake. (Photograph © Pat Ganahl)

Winfield soon determined that the camshaft was the heart of the engine and the key to high performance. By 1925, his own carburetors and cams were being used by the likes of Indy champ Ralph DePalma.

By the close of the 1930s, a small circle of racing-parts manufacturers had developed, including firms such as Offenhauser, Navarro, Eddie Meyer, and Weiand. For the most part, these companies stuck with manufacturing racing hardware, but soon Vic Edelbrock made the important transition of making racing parts available to hot rodders.

Edelbrock was a mechanic by trade and racer by heart, with a seemingly insatiable love for the feel of speed. He had become a consistent winner on Muroc Dry Lake with his roadster, which he drove from the city to the lakes, removing the fenders and windshield, and then running as fast as 121 mph. The idea of a business selling performance parts quickly became obvious. Edelbrock began testing new ideas and combinations of cylinder heads, manifolds, and carburetors. His success was based on his own wisdom, and he was soon enmeshed in creating a line of his own performance parts, including his now-famous twin-carburetor Slingshot manifold and signature racing heads for Ford Flatheads.

THE HOT ROD BOOM

World War II turned hot rodding upside-down. The war drained the nation of so many fine young lives, but at the same time gave the ones who remained a new sense of the future—and they were determined to grasp it firmly. Many of these young men had served in the military or war-related industries, and at the war's end, there was a huge pool of machinists and fabricators in the Los Angeles basin who were skilled in building and wrenching on aircraft, ships, tanks, engines, and more.

Back then, virtually all available parts for improving street performance came from racing equipment. Yet most of the Miller, Frontenac, or Winfield equipment was way out of the price range these young hot rodders could afford. They were left with one choice—figure out how to make it themselves.

In these postwar years, Ed Winfield's work became the inspiration for a young Ed Iskenderian. After serving in the Army Air Corps, Ed returned to Los Angeles and decided that he too would become a cam grinder, just like Winfield and another yet-to-

be-famous cam grinder, Clay Smith. Ed grew tired of waiting for Winfield to grind him cams and so decided to make his own. Ed had spent his teenage years building primitive hot rods, scrounging parts from abandoned Model Ts to build fenderless roadsters, and so believed that making his own cams couldn't be that difficult! Soon, engines running Ed's cams were racing on the Southern California dry lakes, the speedways and streets of Los Angeles, and later in NASCAR, with his Special Iskenderian Racing Cams.

This Californian lust for speed spawned dozens of performance companies bent on going fast. Among the earliest were Belond Headers (Southern California Mufflers Service), Smith & Jones, Spalding Ignition, Tattersfield-Baron, Sharp Speed Equipment, Harmon & Collins, Kong Engineering, Evans & Fenton, and Joe Hunt Magnetos. The first California speed shops—including Blair's Auto Parts, Alex Xydias's So-Cal Speed Shop, and Roy Richter's Bell Auto Parts—all flowered in the postwar years to service the ever-growing interest in hot rodding, lakes racing, and drag racing.

During these same years, several other Southern California hot rod pioneers, like Dean Moon, Robert E. Petersen, and Wally Parks, were also scrambling along the rough and ready road that would lead to the popularity of drag racing, Bonneville land speed racing, street rodding, custom car building, hot rod shows, and even dune buggies.

Dean Moon was a speed-obsessed sixteen-year-old with a bent for raising hell. Important to the fledging sport of hot rodding, his dad owned Moon's Cafe in the hardscrabble oilfields of Santa Fe Springs. Moon's Cafe became a local nerve center where young motorheads from Whittier and other surrounding towns hung out in an extended group of social misfits, dreamers, and racers. In the dusty yard of the café, Dean and his buddies built roadsters and coupes for the street and the dry lakes, an experience that would be Moon's grounding in the creation of hot rod technology.

Another great name also came from the Whittier area. A native son of Denmark, Ak Miller grew up to become a real California kid. He hung out with Moon and built and raced roadsters on the Southern California dry lakes with the Road Runner Car Club before World War II. Ak would later find

Hot Rod Magazine, Vol. 1, No. 1, January 1948

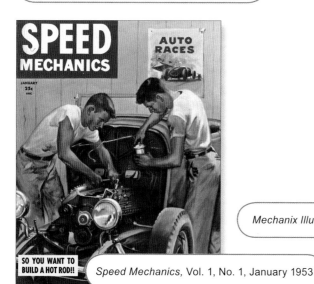

Speed Mechanics, Vol. 1, No. 1, January 1953

Mechanix Illustrated, Vol. 42, No. 2, December 1949

Hot Rodding Magazines:
Journalism on Four Wheels

Some began as timing association newsletters listing club events. Others began as a dream of a single voice for all hot rodders, spreading the good word about race wins and rodding trends.

The most famous of all was Robert E. Petersen's *Hot Rod Magazine*, first published in January 1948. Early issues are quaint, with their simple ads, cute cheesecake pinup photographs, and articles on cars and people that, looking back, now appear larger than life. *Hot Rod* became the flagship of Petersen Publishing Company as well as the single most important rodding magazine then and now.

Other magazines also appeared over time—*Honk!*, *Throttle*, *Hop Up*, *Rod & Custom*, and many more. Hot rodders avidly read most every word in most every issue, the pulp magazines becoming dog-earred and oil-stained proof of their value in disseminating and circulating advice and trends far and wide.

Motor Life, Vol. 3, No. 11, June 1954

Car Craft, Vol. 2, No. 3, July 1954

Rod & Custom, Vol. 2, No. 8, December 1954

Rodding and Re-styling, Vol. 6, No. 11, January 1960

NHRA Tie Rod, Vol. 1, No. 4, March 1956

Drag News, Vol. 3, No. 8, August 10, 1957

fame with his raw road-racing hot rod, the Caballo de Hierro—Horse of Iron—in the Mexican Carrera Panamericana road race, as well as garnering multiple records at both the Bonneville Salt Flats and the Pikes Peak Hillclimb. Ak would develop a mass of advanced hot rod technology for racers for Ford Motor Company. In various guises, he built race cars and hot rods for more than forty years and, in many respects, led the ultimate hot rodder's life.

Another groundbreaking event took place that would forever change the face of hot rodding when "Pete" Petersen introduced the first issue of *Hot Rod Magazine* in January 1948. Even though there were earlier automotive magazines that covered lakes racing, such as *Throttle* and *Speed Age*, *Hot Rod* focused exclusively on hot rodding. The magazine was the seed that would germinate to create an enormous publishing company, Petersen Publishing. Eventually the firm would become the world's premier automotive magazine publisher, with a diverse group of mainstream and special interest titles. And with its influence, the newly issued *Hot Rod Magazine* would help form the National Hot Rodding Association (NHRA) in 1951.

Wally Parks was another child brought to California in the mass exodus from Oklahoma in the 1930s. He arrived in Santa Ana with his parents and two siblings, his teenage years filled with high school and hanging out at Legion Ascot Speedway, Eddie Meyer's race shop, and then with the guys who went dry lakes racing. Parks built street rods and lakes racers, and eventually became the president of the newly formed Southern California Timing Association (SCTA) in 1946 and full-time executive secretary a year later.

Parks and Petersen's acquaintance flowered into life-long friendship through their involvement with the SCTA's first hot rod show, at the Los Angeles Armory in January 1948. As a sideline to this show, Petersen was getting *Hot Rod Magazine* running, and hustling to sell advertising space. Within a short time, Parks became *Hot Rod* editor, and from this powerful position, he would eventually drive both *Hot Rod* and the NHRA to great heights.

During these years, street racing was tearing up the avenues—much to the chagrin of local law enforcement. Parks spread the good word that drag racing was OK—when it was done on a drag strip.

He procured backing with a nationwide drag racing development program, the highly successful Safety Safari that lobbied cities to build drag strips. As editor of *Hot Rod*, he continued his own racing activities, taking class records at Daytona Speed Week in Suddenly, his Plymouth "*Hot Rod Magazine* Special." Today, the NHRA is one of the most recognized racing organizations in the world, running professional drag racing events forty-eight weeks a year. Parks continued on as the NHRA's president for nearly fifty years.

Thanks to Parks, Peterson, and others, hot rodders soon had more places to go fast. In addition to the Southern California dry lakes, racers soon had the National Speed Trials on the Bonneville Salt Flats of Utah to add to their list of yearly events. Parks and Petersen had lobbied state and federal officials to allow hot rodders to use the salt flats annually starting in 1949.

Another pivotal pioneer who emerged out of the street-racing scene was C. J. Hart. A Midwesterner recently arrived in California, Hart was a mechanic by trade. His interest in speed soon spurred him and his newfound hot rodding buddies to race eight-abreast down the airfield at the Orange County Naval Air Station. Ejected from the base, C. J. and two of his racer compatriots, Creighton Hunter and Frank Stillwell, decided to try to legalize this new sport by finding a place to race without military or police harassment. With $1,500 in hand, they approached the Santa Ana Airport managers and came to an agreement to lease one of the unused runways for side-by-side racing on weekends. On June 19, 1950, the Santa Ana Drags opened for business, with the first event bringing in fifty-five entrants and six times that number in spectators. Drag racing was here to stay.

CUSTOM CULTURE

It wasn't just the speed freaks who were making this new hot rod thing happen. The "custom car" guys were also placing their footprint firmly in the history books.

Customs were cars designed for show rather than go. Instead of stripping an automobile down and hot rodding the engine for performance, customs were pure style, paint, and attitude. The custom charge was lead by two brothers, George and Sam Barris.

TRACK T: Dick Jones loves the nostalgic look of old track racers, so he assembled a cool-looking track roadster kit to sell. He built one of his own to promote the kits, painting it brilliant yellow with spectacular flames. The nostalgic look of the Jones Track T follows the style of the Indy Kurtis-Kraft roadsters run at the Brickyard. The main section of the fiberglass roadster body is basically a custom version of a '27 T roadster but the body features a three-piece kit with molded-in doors, trick windscreen installation, lower taillight panel, and opening trunklid. The traditional speedway track nose was fabricated for this rod so it fits around the classic tube-axle torsion-bar front suspension. Designed to use a V6, Dick's car runs a 4.3-liter Chevrolet V6 with a matching four-speed automatic transmission. The engine features Sanderson headers routing the exhaust out the side with a flash of chrome and a nicely aggressive exhaust note. The interior features a hand-formed aluminum tub following the racing heritage behind the Track T concept. (Photograph © David Fetherston)

MR. HORSEPOWER

In the postwar years, Sam and George hooked up in Los Angeles, with George teaching Sam all the tricks he had learned during the early and mid-1940s in various Northern California customs shops. Sam took to this work like a sponge, sucking up every last drop of technique and then blending in his own senses of style and craftsmanship to define a whole new era of American custom cars. The Barris shop soon began turning out stunning customs, such as the Bob Hirohata '51 Mercury; Joe Urritta's Four Foot Ford; Jesse Lopez's '41 Ford, Golden Sahara; Nick Matranga's '41 Mercury Coupe; Larry Ernst's wild '51 Chevy Bel-Air, Kopper Kart; and Bill Carr's Aztec '55 Chevy.

The Barris brothers continued on in business until 1957 when Sam moved to Sacramento. George stayed on in Southern California to create an empire of customs, hot rods, and movie cars spanning more than sixty years. George set and broke so many barriers that his ideas fueled much of custom car culture. George continued to make his mark crafting such fabulous rods as the Emperor, Twister T, and the Surf Woody, while creating a long line of movie cars from the Batmobile to the Munster Koach and Beverly Hillbillies truck. And he not only built cars but also labored as a show promoter, writer, photographer, movie maker, and all-round trendsetter.

As history has so clearly proven, the Barris shop was not just about George. He provided an opportunity for others to flourish as well, including pinstripers Von Dutch and Dean Jeffries; streamliner builder "Jocko" Johnson; world-famous custom car painter Hershel "Junior" Conway, later of Junior's House of Color fame; car builders Dick Dean, Richard "Korky" Korkes, Lyle Lake, and Bill Hines; and even *Street Rodder* magazine publisher Tom McMullen. They were all part of the Barris shop crew at one time or another.

There were other significant custom builders emerging too. Gene Winfield was doing amazing work at Winfield's Custom Shop in Modesto, and Joe Bailon in Hayward was creating spectacular customs such as Miss Elegance, the Mystery Ford, and Scoopy Doo. By the mid-1950s, Dean Jeffries was the leader of a new generation of custom car masters. After apprenticing with Barris, Jeffries opened his own shop, building quality rods and customs, and winning the prestigious Grand National Roadster Show Tournament of Fame with his Ford-powered Manta Ray in 1964. Dean would go on to create the wild GTO custom Monkeemobile for *The Monkees* TV show, and the custom Imperial for the Green Hornet.

Another new custom craftsman was Bill Cushenbery. Bill opened shop in Wichita, Kansas, but quickly moved to Monterey, California in 1958. There he built wild customs and custom rods such as the Matador, Tony Cardoza's outrageous '59 Impala custom, and later, the Car Craft Dream Rod and Ford Astro.

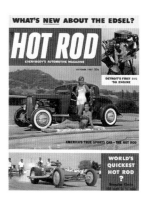

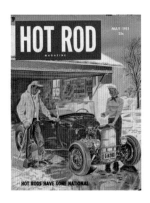

CLASSIC COUPE: Bill Turner owned this '32 five-window coupe for quite a time and cruised with the Road Zombies Car Club. The classic coupe features small bobbed fenders with Buick brakes, 350 Chevy engine, and Turbo 400 automatic transmission. The steel wheels painted in bright gloss red richly offset the flat-black primered paintwork and the wide-whitewalled tires, which offer up a clean tight look with the chrome beauty rings. The interior was trimmed in black-and-white tuck-and-roll, in true hot rod fashion. (Photograph © David Fetherston)

Custom car culture was not all West Coast action. The Alexander brothers, Mike and Larry, started out in Detroit on their path to custom Nirvana, painting in a wooden, one-stall garage in the mid-1950s. The brothers went on to build earthshaking customs, including the Alexa Ford, the Adonis, "Chilli" Catallo's Little Deuce Coupe, and the definitive Dodge Deora, which is considered by many today as the ultimate custom.

Several legendary characters emerged out of the early 1950s, growing larger than life in later years. Kenneth Howard, a.k.a. Von Dutch, became a famed pinstriper. While his true relevance to the history of hot rodding may have been mystic, he became a cultural icon.

Another pinstriper took the wild and crazy side of hot rodding and turned it on its head. Ed "Big Daddy" Roth led a rich and diverse life through fifty years of hot rodding. An inventor, sculptor, painter, striper, artist, car builder, engineer, and all-round crazy guy, Roth defined the idea of "thinking outside the box" before the phrase itself became a cliché.

Ed's early years were spent street racing, cruising, and hanging out at the Clock Drive-In in Bell, California and the Hula-Hut, with the likes of Dean Moon and the Chrisman brothers. After an Air Force tour of duty in the early 1950s, Ed returned to make a life-long business of being "Big Daddy." His journey started when he hooked up with Bud Croizer, who went by the nickname "Baron." The pair opened shop in Southgate as Baron and Roth, launching zany airbrushed T-shirts and pinstriping and painting rods with scallops and flames. This partnership moved Ed from custom painting to building rods. During these years, he also created his Rat Fink character, evolving from a swiggle on a napkin to hot rodding's own wild cartoon madman. Through the years, Ed championed Rat Fink as "Mickey Mouse's crazy brother."

Roth eventually got serious about doing what he considered art, and through a life full of up and downs, he eventually turned out a long series of groundbreaking and artistic hot rods. In his usual way, Ed took his own path, designing and building his Outlaw like no other hot rod ever created. He sculpted the bodywork, made a mold, and built it out of fiberglass. Outlaw was quickly followed by Beatnik Bandit, Tweedy Pie, Mysterion, Road Agent, Orbitron, Surfite, Druid Princess, Globe Hooper, and more. Ed also went racing for a time when he got involved in building and campaigning the famous Yellow Fang Top Fuel dragster with George "Bushmaster" Schreiber. In an unexpected twist of fate, his hot rods became some of Revell's most popular model toy kits during the 1960s. But Ed found discomfort with this corporate involvement. He returned to pinstriping in the 1970s and 1980s, only to find a huge revival of interest in his life's work in the 1990s. In April 2001, just as Big Daddy was finally getting the creative and cultural recognition he so deserved, he passed away.

THE EVOLUTION OF HOT RODDING

By the mid-1960s, hot rodding was evolving into street rodding just as Andy Brizio was introducing his Andy's Instant T, a Model T kit rod. This Instant T presented an opportunity for guys to build a drivable hot rod at home without having to hunt through junkyards for an eternity in search of impossible-to-find parts. Now, thirty-five years later, Andy's son Roy runs the fabulous Roy Brizio Street Rods in South San Francisco.

As the mid-1960s moved into the early 1970s, the availability of parts to build hot rods evolved from a few suspension parts like dropped axles, custom wheels, and chromed engine accessories to the manufacture of every part of a hot rod, including dozens of body variations. Nowadays, a Deuce Coupe can be built from all-new parts while still retaining the spirit of 1932.

The past forty years has seen hot rodding evolve, crash, and then rise again and mature. The hot rodding and custom world today boasts amazing talents grasping every aspect of the sport, from custom fabrications to great shows and events, glorious new paint finishes to new performance options, billet wheels on down to rat rods. The movement has been driven by a talent pool of movers and shakers, including Gray Baskerville, Boyd Coddington, Gary Meadors of Goodguys fame, Pete and Jake, Posies, Troy Trepanier, Sam and Chip Foose, "Fat Jack" Robinson, Alan Johnson, and Roy Brizio. These folks and so many others are part of what is now a multimillion dollar hot rod business.

The PATRON SAINTS
of Hot Rodding

By Steve Hendrickson

Steve Hendrickson has been surrounded by hot rods since childhood, when his dad was involved in circle track racing. In the '70s, his entire family got involved in street rodding, traveling all over the Upper Midwest in a '38 Chevy coupe and camping at events. Cars turned into a career when he was hired as an editor for *Street Rodder* magazine in 1985. A few years later, he went to work for *Rodder's Digest* magazine, and he's had several articles published in the *Hop Up* annuals. He currently works for *CarTech,* publishing high-performance how-to books and racing histories.

Steve's garage is filled to overflowing with an autocrossing '60 Austin-Healey Sprite, an original '54 Chevy pickup, and a '50s-style '32 Ford three-window hot rod. He likes long walks in junkyards and curling up by the fire with a nice speed equipment catalog, and he believes there is an as-yet-undefined relationship between Zen and gas welding.

FOR THE PATRON SAINT OF NOSTALGIA: During the dark days of the early 1970s, George Lucas' coming-of-age film *American Graffiti* revived America's love affair with hot rodding. The movie was stuffed with classic cars, from stocks to rods and customs, including a white Thunderbird '58 custom Chevy Impala, the black '55 Chevy, and John Milner's chopped yellow '32 five-window, which went on to become one of the most famous hot rods of all time.

Every movement, every class, every little group of humanity that ever banded together for a common interest has had its founding fathers—people who had a hand in forming that group's identity and keeping it on track. Hot rodding is no exception. In the fifty or sixty years since the sport really got going, we've had our share of notable characters. Luckily, most of them are still with us today.

Here then are the ten patron saints of hot rodding. Some of them have had positions of influence, most haven't. But all of them have showed us, in one way or another, what it is to be a hot rodder.

TOM MEDLEY: PATRON SAINT OF HUMOR

Tom is a legitimate hot rodding legend—and doesn't seem to know it. One of the first staffers of *Hot Rod Magazine*, he stayed with Peterson Publishing for more than forty years and was instrumental in turning *Rod & Custom* magazine back to traditional street-based hot rodding in the late '60s. It's even come to light in recent years that he and Tex Smith finagled the funding for the first Street Rod Nationals, which led to the National Street Rod Association and the formation of a nationwide street rod movement from the '70s to today.

But most important, Tom's unassuming demeanor and quick wit also created Stroker McGurk, the Hot Rodder's Buddy. In the first issue of *Hot Rod*, Tom was listed as Cartoons and Humor Editor, and that issue contained a couple of cartoons by him. The main character was always a hot rodder, usually dressed in a rakish driving cap. The first Stroker McGurk cartoon ran in April '48, and was a regular feature for years after. Tom and Stroker taught us not to take ourselves too seriously, and we'll be forever in their debt.

WALLY PARKS: PATRON SAINT OF BURNOUTS

As the first editor of *Hot Rod*, Wally literally defined hot rodding. His first editorial said that hot rodders were "interested in automobiles whose engines and bodies have been rebuilt in the quest for better performance and appearance." The definition stands today, whether you're talking about a traditional '29 Ford roadster on Deuce rails, or a Honda Civic with an Integra B18C engine swap and nitrous.

Through the pages of *Hot Rod*, Wally organized hot rodders, and in the course of a few years, he created the National Hot Rod Association and completely reversed the public's perception of hot rods and hot rodders. In the ensuing years, he brought together drag racers and drag racing under one national banner. Of course, NHRA and drag racing went off in a different direction from what we today think of as

hot rodding, but Wally never forgot his roots. The NHRA Hot Rod Reunion and the NHRA Museum in Pomona (now named for Wally) are proof of that.

TEX SMITH: PATRON SAINT OF BENCHRACING

Leroi "Tex" Smith has been part of the hot rodding scene almost since Day One, and has stories to tell about everything and everyone. He's worked on *Hot Rod*, *Rod & Custom*, *Street Rodder*, *Rod Action*, his own *Hot Rod Mechanix*, and probably a few other magazines that we can't remember. His book-publishing company gave us some of the best hot rod grassroots how-to books ever put together (it still exists as The Hot Rod Library), and he's played an integral part in the formation of just about everything related to hot rodding today.

He's now enjoying a well-earned retirement, fishing for salmon with his buddies, building hot rods, traveling the world, and just generally being Tex. Tex never seemed to stay put long, and despite the fact that not all of his publishing enterprises were successful, there are few people we'd rather share a beer with. It's simply impossible not to like Tex.

BOYD CODDINGTON: PATRON SAINT OF BILLET

In the early '80s, a former Disneyland machinist started turning out some special cars from his small shop in Stanton, California. The cars were exceptionally well crafted with many handbuilt components, using a lot of custom-machined billet-aluminum parts. The guy was Boyd Coddington, and when the magazines started featuring his work, well-heeled and loyal customers formed a line. A new movement in street rodding was born.

Boyd's cars weren't just built, they were designed and fabricated, often completely from scratch. The first billet wheels showed up on his cars, and that led to a second wheel-building business that revolutionized our rolling stock.

Boyd founded a look and a business empire that eventually crumbled under its own monumental weight. But Mr. Coddington proved to be tough enough to beat that setback, and today a leaner, meaner Boyd is back with a vengeance, building cutting-edge hot rods, making the coolest wheels, and leaving behind more aluminum chips in the process.

Boyd took hot rodding uptown, and his companies were instrumental in bringing the hobby to a new audience and in increasing its legitimacy. He also built some damn cool cars in the process, and you can bet that he and his influence will be around for a long time to come.

PETE CHAPOURIS: PATRON SAINT OF MAIL ORDER

As one of the founders of Pete & Jake's Hot Rod Parts, Pete Chapouris saw a need for simple, high-quality chassis parts that hot rodders could buy and bolt on. What started as Pete & Jake's Hot Rod Repair soon turned into Pete & Jake's Hot Rod Parts, and their catalog included a wealth of chassis and suspension components that any hot rodder could install in his or her own garage.

Pete was also the owner and builder of one of the most famous hot rods of all time—The California Kid—which starred in a Martin Sheen TV movie of the same name. It was a black-with-flames '34 Ford coupe that, along with the *American Graffiti* '32 Ford, helped relight the fire of hot rodding in the early '70s.

After the boys from Temple City sold their business, Pete kept building high-profile cars, eventually teaming up with Alex Xydias to recreate the So-Cal Speed Shop—a business that seems to have as much influence on Ford, Chrysler, and General Motors as it does on hot rodders.

Pete and Jake were pioneers of the street rod industry, and their success led others to try the market as well. Today, we can buy parts off the shelf to build dozens of complete cars, including all-steel '32 Ford roadsters. Some of you might say that store-bought cars aren't real hot rods, but remember, these parts have made it possible for thousands of people to build cars and have fun with them. And fun with cars is what hot rodding is all about.

JIM "JAKE" JACOBS: PATRON SAINT OF PRIMER

Despite the fact that he's half of the most famous duo in hot rodding, Jim has always been a low-key, unassuming guy who knows exactly what it takes to make a hot rod right.

Jake was also a part of the *Rod & Custom* staff in the late '60s, an integral part of the team that turned the magazine away from mini-bikes, go-karts, and other foo-fraw and back to traditional hot rodding.

Right, *OLD FLAMES:* A forgotten flamed custom and Deuce coupe rest in peace in front of the Evergreen Drive-In Theater in this painting by automotive artist Dale Klee. (Artwork © Dale Klee)

Following pages, **ROAD ROCKETS:** A lineup of hot rods and customs waits outside the Road Rockets Motel in this painting by artist and hot rodder Kent Bash. (Artwork © Kent Bash)

If you get a chance, find some of those magazines and take a look at his work—the stories, photos, and illustrations are a part of his natural talent that many don't remember.

Jake was way ahead of his time when he found and restored the Niekamp Roadster (the first Oakland winner). These days, his own cars are practically legends. That list includes his yellow '34 coupe (a sibling to The California Kid), the cross-country '29 Model A pickup, and a very nice Model A panel truck, among others.

Our favorite was his Jakester, the '29 Model A tub which, at the height of the billet-and-smoothie craze, had red brush paint, 16-inch steelies, and genuine Indian blankets for upholstery. Actually, the car's first finish was a natural iron-oxide patina. He and a bunch of friends painted it red at the Goodguys's Pleasanton Nats. Later, Jake decoupaged the car with old *Hot Rod Magazine*s. The car was as basic and down-to-earth as you could get, and it showed a lot of people that it doesn't have to be done to be fun.

GARY MEADORS: PATRON SAINT OF FAIRGROUNDS

Gary got his event-building career started with the NSRA, where his laidback style and good humor earned him the nickname Goodguy. In '87, though, he struck out on his own, forming the Goodguys Rod & Custom Association. Today, their annual schedule includes twenty-two events from coast to coast.

So what's so special about a bunch of events? Goodguys events have an energy that's hard to define. Perhaps it's because these events allow later-model cars (cut-off dates vary from 1954 to 1972). It's always nice to see customs, street machines, muscle cars, and other later iron mixing it up with the hot rods . . . and the ideas tend to flow both ways. Then again, it might be that several Goodguys events include drag racing—the nostalgia dragsters are always fun to watch, and a lot of hot rodders started taking their street iron to the strip as well.

THOM TAYLOR: PATRON SAINT OF DREAMERS

Thom draws 'em, we build 'em. Few illustrators have had Thom's ability to spot, create, or develop hot rod styling trends. His imaginative sketches have

Pendleton's Speed Custom Shop
SHELBY, N.C.

ESTABLISHED 1948
WORLD FAMOUS
HONEST CHARLEY™
SPEED SHOP
CHATTANOOGA, TENN.

Ball
ROD & KUSTOM
Syracuse, Indiana
(219) 457-2880

SUN AUTOMOTIVE
PERFORMANCE SPECIALTIES

CAL CUSTOM

BELL AUTO PARTS
RACING EQUIPMENT
BELL, CALIFORNIA

HOLLYWOOD
11421 Santa Monica Blvd.
Los Angeles 25, Calif.
HOT ROD SHOP

SO-CAL SPEED SHOP

HALL'S
SPEED SHOP
WICHITA
Established 1948

ROCCO & CHEATERS
SPEED SHOP
BIRMINGHAM
316 First Ave. N.
Phone 322-8461, 324-1931

So-Cal
SPEED SHOP

MANHATTAN SPEED
232 West Broadway
New York, N.Y. 10013
CA 6-5016-17
POWER EQUIPMENT

Tornado
SPEED
EQUIPMENT
TORNADO
BLOWS 'EM
ALL OFF!
LEE'S SPEED SHOP
1743 EAST 14TH STREET OAKLAND, CALIF. TEmplebar 4-9964

AUTOMOTIVE PERFORMANCE PRODUCTS
SPEED
SPECIALTIES
13517 Santa Monica Blvd.
W. Los Angeles, Calif.
90025
FOR TOP SPEED AND POWER

SCHLIEPER'S
SPEED SHOP
RACING ENGINES
and
EQUIPMENT
2-7950
2985 N. BARKER RD.
BROOKFIELD, WIS.

Facing page, **HOT ROD SPEED SHOP DECALS**

Right, **LEAN:** Rat rods come in all forms of body styles, from pickups to coupes to roadsters—and even some two-door sedans. However, they don't get much simpler or leaner than this severely chopped and channeled roadster. It features all the right touches: an early OHV GM powertrain tricked out with some simple fifties speed equipment, polished engine accessories, dump headers, Moon discs, whitewalls, and a severely chopped aftermarket Du-Vall-style cast windshield. This roadster personifies the wildest street rods to hit the blacktop in the pioneering years of hot rodding. (Photograph © David Fetherston)

graced almost every hot rod magazine out there, and many of his cars have been transferred to 3-D and 1:1 scale by such talented builders as Ken Fenical, Boyd Coddington, Greg Fluery, and others. Thom has also done styling work for real automakers, influencing our daily drivers as well.

GEORGE LUCAS: PATRON SAINT OF DRIVE-INS

The late '60s were dark days for hot rodding. Vans, dune buggies, go-karts, muscle cars, and other sinister, distractive forces nearly drove our beloved '29 Hi-Boy roadsters and their kin to extinction. But in 1973, a young filmmaker, George Lucas, put together *American Graffiti*, a coming-of-age film set in 1962 in a small California town. John Milner, his '32 five-window, Mel's Drive-In, and the other characters and cars in that movie are now cultural icons. That movie got a lot of guys thinking about those good old days, and many of them realized that the time was right to relive them once again.

AL TEAGUE: PATRON SAINT OF SALT

Four hundred and nine miles per hour, with a single-piston engine, driving two wheels. By himself. That's our definition of a hot rodding hero, and it's Al Teague.

Al's current car, named Spirit of '76, was built by him in '75 and first ran in 1976. Since then, the car has been upgraded and altered many times, and it has set records all along the way. Currently the full-bodied lakester is powered by an aluminum hemi, and holds the Federation International de l'Automobile land speed record of 409.986 mph for piston-engine, wheel-driven cars. On one of the runs that produced that record average, Teague was clocked at 432 mph.

He's not just the fastest hot rodder in the world, Al's also one of the nicest and most down-to-earth people you'll ever meet. One day at the Fremont Nostalgia Nats in '86, two friends of ours were having trouble packing the 'chute on their front-engine digger. Some guy came by and offered to help, showed them how to hook up the rubber bands, wrap the cords, and get it all together right. They thanked him, and when he left, one turned to the other and said, "Do you know who that was?"

The other, slack-jawed, said, "Uh-huh."

The first replied, "You just had your 'chute packed by God!"

Turns out "God" was Al Teague.

You can have your Craig Breedloves and your Richard Nobles; they might be faster, but real hot rodders know that jet cars are for pussies. Al Teague is the real deal.

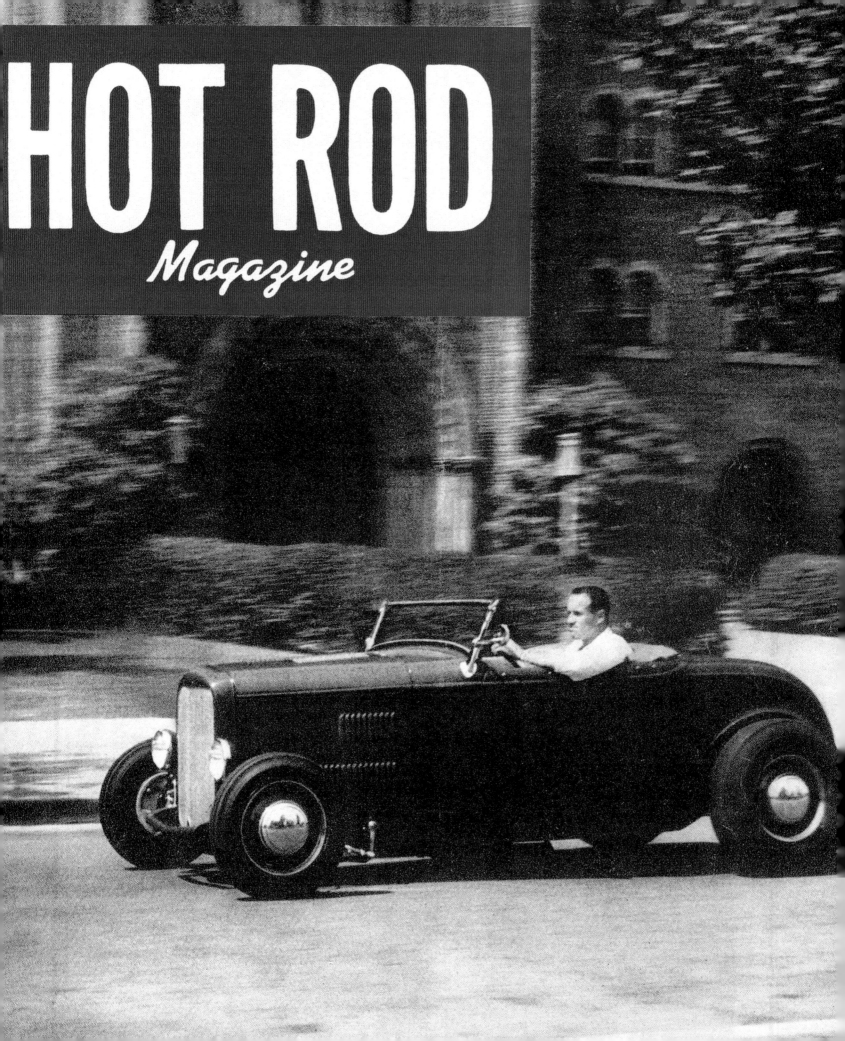

HOT ROD
Magazine

20 That Counted

By Pat Ganahl

Pat Ganahl grew up in California and never left his love of surfing, guitar playing, and hot rodding behind. As an editor, writer, and photographer, he keeps these flames alive today.

Along the road, Pat has become one of the most respected and knowledgeable journalists concerning hot rods and custom cars. He is well known among buffs as the past editor of such magazines as *Hot Rod*, *Rod & Custom*, *Street Rodder*, and *The Rodder's Journal*. He's also the author of numerous books, including, most recently, *Ed "Big Daddy" Roth: His Life, Times, Cars*, and *Art and Von Dutch: The Art, The Myth, The Legend*.

Who better, then, to look back and assess twenty of the most influential hot rods of all time? Pat's greatest hits is a personal list, but then hot rodding is a supremely personal artform.

BOB MCGEE–DICK SCRITCHFIELD '32 ROADSTER: The Hi-Boy Deuce belonged to University of Southern California football star Bob McGee when it hit the cover of *Hot Rod* in October 1948. (Pat Ganahl collection)

Ace rock-guitarist Steve Vai said not long ago that you can't name the best guitar player in the world because, first of all, it's an art, and art can't really be judged. Second, there are many different styles of playing, and someone would have to master all of them to be considered the best, which will never happen.

Although it's a loose analogy, judging hot rods is similar.

In the first place, by definition, a hot rod is a vehicle built to reflect the owner's taste, style, or whims. There is a general consensus, of course, about which styles are better than others. But the hallmark of hot rodding is individuality and creativity. Setting a new trend is as good as perfecting an older or existing one.

Secondly, hot rods are built for a variety of purposes, including several types of racing, competing at car shows, vying for attention (or trophies) at weekend rod runs or in magazine pages, or just for driving around and having fun. Also, today, for the first time in their history, certain hot rods are being considered classics of the genre and are actually being restored and displayed in such things as museums and concours gatherings.

So (although I have done it in the past), I will not presume here to name the Top 20 Hot Rods, or some selection of the All-Time Best. Instead I present twenty hot rods that were either outstanding for their time; trendsetting in one way or another; highly popular with the rodding public or influential because of magazine, movie, or other media exposure; or which just plain epitomize a style of rodding for a given era or for all time. The following examples are presented in more or less chronological order, and a surprising number of them have been restored or preserved and have found their way into museums or similar collections.

ED ISKENDERIAN'S '23 T ROADSTER

Ed Iskenderian, or Isky, is known to legions of rodders and racers as The Camfather. He learned how to grind camshafts on his own, and built his own machinery to do it. As a high school student at Manual Arts in Los Angeles after World War II, when he was learning these crafts, souping up old cars was highly popular and he and a couple of friends decided to compete to see who could build the best roadster. Isky may have won out (though his friend John Athan's was driven by Elvis in *Loving You* and is also in a museum). With a set of Essex frame rails, a discarded Model T body, a relatively new Ford V8 engine he found in a junkyard, and a pair of similarly accessed '34 Pontiac grilles (the top halves of which he welded together to make one smooth, oval unit), he had this sleek, black-lacquered roadster on the road by '38 or '39.

Like most hot rods, it evolved over a period of time, including additions like the grille, a rare set of Maxi F-heads (for which he cast his own aluminum, engraved valve covers), triple carburetors, handmade chromed exhaust pipes, the engine-turned firewall, an expertly crafted oxblood leather interior, and such

Facing page, **ED ISKEN-DERIAN'S '23 T ROAD-STER**

Isky saves everything— and that includes his old T roadster. Stored in a back room at the Isky Cams shop, it was simply dusted off for this photo in the early 1990s. It was later brought out of seclusion for a gallery show at Art Center College in 1993, and has been in museums since. The flying skull grille ornament was one of several cast at Manual Arts High in the 1930s. (Photograph © Robert Kittila)

Right, top, **DOANE SPENCER '32 FORD ROADSTER:**

Doane being presented the Best Appearing Car trophy by none other than SCTA President Wally Parks and Vice President Ak Miller in the Rose Bowl parking lot at the first Pasadena Reliability Run in 1947. (Pat Ganahl collection)

Right, bottom, **BILL NIEKAMP ROADSTER:**

The NieKamp roadster was likely the first hot rod restored to its original form, done by Jim Jacobs in 1970. Here it is seen with headlights removed for further streamlining as it competed at the lakes in the '50s. (Photograph © Pat Ganahl)

high-end touches as Cadillac pedals and aircraft gauges. But, after running more than 110 mph at the dry lakes, it appeared in its finished form on the June 1948 cover of *Hot Rod Magazine* and has, quite literally, not been touched since.

DOANE SPENCER'S '32 FORD ROADSTER

First of all, his name was Doane (not Duane). His club was the Stokers of Glendale (not Strokers). And his smooth, glossy black, fast Deuce fell equally out of step with hot roadsters of the immediate postwar period, all in good ways. Few such hot rods (as they were just then starting to be called) could boast a better-than-factory, hand-rubbed lacquer paint job. Nor a leather interior with a pull-down center armrest pirated from a '40s Cadillac. Nor the rare, custom-made DuVall V-windshield. Other Spencer-crafted components included

the solid hood, a rounded cover for the rear gas tank with an inset license plate and teardrop '37 Ford taillights on either side, the "hairpin" front radius rods, and a unique headlight-mounting "nerf" bar. Doane even hand-formed a lift-off steel hardtop for the car, though he seldom used it.

In this form, Doane drove the car cross-country several times, raced it on the dry lakes (and streets), and kept changing it in small ways. Around 1950, he tore the car apart, fabricated a ground-clearing exhaust that exited through the frame rails, and was installing a big Lincoln OHV V8 in preparation for running the fabled Mexican Road Race. But within a year or two that race was terminated, and the roadster sat in pieces.

In the '70s, Los Angeles Roadsters member Neal East acquired it and drove it in a beautiful street rod version (with a flathead V8), and more recently collector Bruce Meyer had it restored to a '50s version, which won first place at the historic inaugural hot rod class at the Pebble Beach Concours in 1997.

BOB MCGEE–DICK SCRITCHFIELD'S '32 ROADSTER

As seen on the October 1948 cover of *Hot Rod* when it belonged to University of Southern California football star Bob McGee, this red roadster was known as the lowest of the Hi-Boys, due to its deeply C-ed rear frame rails. In this form it duly competed at the

dry lakes and was displayed at the first Southern California Timing Association Hot Rod Show at the Los Angeles Armory in 1948 (where no trophies were awarded).

The car gained significantly more exposure and fame during the decades it was owned by Los Angeles Roadsters founding father Dick Scritchfield, beginning in 1956. Not only did it receive one of the first Chevy V8 transplants and one of the first (short-lived) metalflake paint jobs, but it also starred in numerous movies, commercials, and TV shows, including the curb-running, hubcap-banging opening scene of *Hot Rod Gang.* Of course, it led hundreds of early rod runs and posed for countless magazine articles in its

yellow, red, and black paint versions, not to mention setting a C/Street Roadster record of 167+ mph at Bonneville in 1971.

Today it has been restored to the '40s McGee version by Bruce Meyer, who displays it at the Petersen Automotive Museum.

BILL NIEKAMP'S ROADSTER

Bill NieKamp was a painter at the Los Angeles Chrysler plant when he built his low-slung '29 A roadster, which accounts for the unflattering pastel blue color—he used free Dodge paint. But the sensuous Whitey Clayton track nose, three-piece hood, belly pans, and other streamlining bodywork (over '27

Essex frame rails) were enough to earn this car the first big America's Most Beautiful Roadster (AMBR) trophy at the inaugural Oakland Roadster Show in 1950. It also accounted for high speeds at the dry lakes—a primary intent, since NieKamp was a racer at heart.

The car was found in the late '60s by then-*Rod & Custom* staffer Jim Jacobs (later of Pete & Jake's fame), who decided to return it to its 1950 con-figuration, just because that's the way he thought it should be. In this flathead-powered form he drove it cross-country to early NSRA "Nats" and on countless other trips and rod runs, eventually installing a more reliable Chevy engine. By '97 he restored it again to flathead form for the Pebble Beach show, and it has since been acquired by a private collector.

NORM WALLACE'S ROADSTER

For some still-unexplained reason, when hot rodding spread to the East Coast and Midwest after World War II, builders in those regions preferred the chan-neled look, in which the floor was cut out, the body was dropped low over the frame, and then the floor was re-attached higher, affording little legroom but a very low overall stance. This was obviously done after the stock fenders were removed, and it was done to (usually unchopped) coupes as well as roadsters. Some of the better-known such rods include Tommy Foster's blue Deuce roadster from the Midwest, and Andy Kassa's '32 coupe and Bill Neuman's red road-ster from the East.

One of the nicest of these cars, however, was Norm Wallace's flathead-powered, Titian Maroon Deuce roadster from Dover, New Hampshire, which was a regular winner at the prestigious Hartford Autorama, and was finally featured in *Hot Rod* in September 1958. This car survived in relatively unchanged form for years. With only the addition of a S.CO.T. super-charger, it was acquired by Larry Hook of Providence, Rhode Island, about a decade ago, and was shown at Pebble Beach in '99.

JOE NITTI'S HI-BOY ROADSTER

Joe Nitti's clean '32 Ford Hi-Boy roadster was featured on one page in the June 1950 *Hot Rod*, simply titled Deep Purple '32. As far as I know, it was never fea-tured in any other magazine, it was never shown in color, and it never won any major awards or set any

speed records (though it was raced at El Mirage; Nitti belonged to the Vultures club of the Russetta Timing Association). But there's something about this car that has captured every warm-blooded hot rodder's fancy. It's late '40s, early '50s period perfect. It has all the right stuff.

From the '39 Ford teardrop taillights in back to the chromed and V-ed (possibly the first) spreader bar in front, this car epitomizes a rod of the golden era—big and little wide whites with baby moons, filled and peaked grille shell, chopped windshield, solid hood punched with hot rod louvers, white tuck and roll. All of us could see the rich, glass-like purple in those black and white photos. The fact that Nitti was sponsored by a chrome shop certainly didn't hurt.

After it disappeared fifty years ago, someone recently found the Nitti car, had it quickly restored, and now it seems to be gone again.

DICK FLINT'S ROADSTER

There's one thing about this streamlined '29 Model A roadster with the distinctive track-style nose—you either love it or hate it. Most rodders love it, and it just happened to star on one of *Hot Rod Magazine*'s kitschiest, campiest covers of the early '50s (May 1952, to be exact).

With unusual body panels formed by Valley Cus-tom, it made all the magazines of the day. And its streamlining was more than visual: fitted with an Edelbrock-built flathead, it turned more than 143 mph at the dry lakes—then an incredible time for a regularly street-driven roadster.

After yeoman duty as tour-leader for the Los Ange-les Roadsters, with a Chevy engine and dilapidating frame when Duane Kofoed owned it in the '60s and '70s, it underwent a lengthy do-and-redo restoration

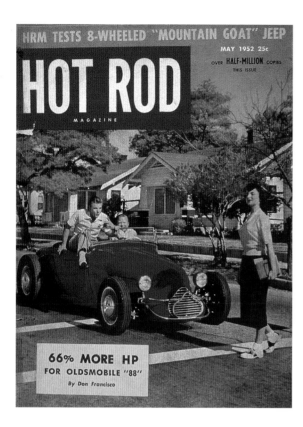

process throughout the '90s before finally winning the second Pebble Beach hot rod roadster class for present owner Don Orosco in 1999.

EDDIE DYE'S ROADSTER

Little is known about this gorgeous, track-nosed Model A roadster, other than the fact it was featured on the cover of the short-lived *Hop Up* magazine (March 1952, the last black and white cover). It was built by Gil and Al Ayala, the East Los Angeles less-heralded counterparts to the Barris brothers. It's an example of one of the Ayalas' few hot rod projects, as opposed to customs. They completely smoothed and filled the '29 body, including welding the doors shut, and covered the Deuce frame with bellypans before hand-forming the beautiful nose and hood panels. The Vee windshield is from George DuVall. Although the magazine copy neglects to state the car's color, it says the engine is a full-house flatty by Earl Evans (though shown neither in photos nor in a full cutaway drawing).

Sometime in the '60s, this car was stripped of its nose, hood, and windshield, fitted with a Chevy engine and mag wheels, and painted gold. In this form, it appeared briefly in an era teen flick, then reappeared in the late '90s. Today, the car exists in two "restored"

versions: one with the original body and chassis with a reproduced nose; the other with the real hood and nose but a different Model A body.

THE KOOKIE KAR

Model T-bodied hot rods existed since well before the term "hot rod" was coined (Isky's is just one). But Norm Grabowski's raked, shortened, flamed, Cad-powered, and many-piped '23 roadster, with its chopped grille and top and sawed-off pickup bed, engendered a fad that persists today. Appropriately named "Fad T's," they were the rod du jour of the '70s, reproduced by the hundreds, if not thousands, in fiberglass.

After first appearing on *Hot Rod*'s cover in black and white in '55, it was wrecked and rebuilt on a jauntier angle with a suicide front end before being shown at Bob's drive-in on a full page in *Life* magazine in '57. Of course, it made the car magazine covers too, in its blue-and-flamed version. But it was as comb-wielding Kookie's car on TV's *77 Sunset Strip* from 1958 to 1960 that it made a whole new generation yearn to own a hot rod "just like that one"–and many eventually did.

TOMMY IVO'S T

Whereas Grabowski's T got famous in Hollywood and led to an acting career for its owner, Tommy Ivo started as a child actor, fell in love with cars, duplicated the Kookie T, took it to the strip, and ended up a career drag racer. But that's just a side note.

What's important to us is that after scrutinizing and even measuring Grabowski's T (Norm caught him doing it), Ivo refined the T-bucket rod style. While the Kookie Kar's strength is that it's all colors and components akimbo, Ivo's–though still a wild rod–has a more proportionate stance, a symmetry to its Buick's pipes and injectors, and a striking white-over-red theme to the whole car. Surprisingly, while Norm's frenetic flames and stripes were done by Dean Jeffries, Ivo's much more traditional striping was applied by the usually outrageous Von Dutch.

Ivo's T starred equally on screen and the quarter mile for a year or two, before Bill Rolland got it and over-refined it. Meanwhile "TV Tom" enjoyed several successful decades in dragsters, Funny Cars, and jet cars. Now his historic T has finally been restored and resides in the NHRA Motorsport Museum.

Left, **DICK FLINT ROADSTER:** The esteemed Valley Custom shop pounded out the unusual nose, hood, and bellypans on this rapid red roadster, while Flint himself made the chrome tube nerf bars and other details. Note the inverted louvers. (Pat Ganahl collection)

Facing page, top, **NORM GRABOWSKI'S KOOKIE KAR:** Hot rods had been wild machines from the outset, but before Norm Grabowski came up with this exuberant mélange of pipes, carbs, flames, and a bleeding-skull shift knob, nothing like this had come down the pike. Can you imagine how John Q. Public reacted when he saw this on a full page in *Life* magazine in 1957. While the original still exists, Franco Costanza built this exact replica in the late 1980s. (Photograph © Pat Ganahl)

Right, **EDDIE DYE ROADSTER:** Dye built this roadster up from a Ford Model A. The '52 magazine feature on the car doesn't tell its color, but it looks like a deep metallic in the photo. (Pat Ganahl collection)

BOB McCOY'S FORTY

If you've been counting, you've noticed that the first half of these twenty significant rods have been roadsters, and '32 or earlier model Fords, at that. If you know hot rods, this shouldn't surprise you. Early rods were all roadsters, and most were Fords. In fact, in my opinion, the term "hot rod" derives from "roadster." That's a discussion for another time.

But by the '50s, coupes—and even sedans—were competing for attention as well as other things. Bob McCoy's flamed Forty from San Diego was hardly the first, but it is one of the most remembered and revered by all rodders. I'm not sure why.

There's not all that much done to the car. The highly polished black paint, in fact, was factory original. The red-yellow-orange warbird nose flames were nothing new, but they sure set this car off. So did the white-and-black full tuck-and-roll interior (probably done in nearby Tijuana). It had a hot, full-race flat-

head under the hood. And it sat on a good rake. But, for a big, fat-fendered sedan, it said *hot rod* loud and clear. That must have been it. Then it was gone.

TOM POLLARD'S '29 ROADSTER

This car doesn't make many Top 20 lists, but it should. It was featured on major magazine covers no less than four times in the mid-'50s, beginning in an all-

red form on *Rod & Custom* in August '54, then on a full *Hot Rod* cover with TV's *Dragnet* star Jack Webb in January '55. But even before that cover appeared, George Barris convinced Pollard to repaint his car a bright metallic lime green so he could add frenetic burgundy flames over a new three-piece hood, down

over the molded-in '40 DeLuxe dash, and from small louvers stamped in new cycle fenders.

In the meantime, Barris had painted George Sein's '32 coupe in an opposite color scheme, with lots of striping by Dean Jeffries, and he arranged for these cars to be displayed side-by-side in a special area at the 1954 Los Angeles Motorama car show. Not only that, but Pollard's freshly painted roadster was striped by the inimitable Von Dutch right there, to the delight of show spectators. Although it didn't appear until a couple years later, the June '57 *Car Craft* cover, featuring Pollard's and Sein's rods together, remains one of the all-time classic rod magazine covers.

The car, surprisingly, does exist today, in an older, more sedate lime-green-and-flamed paint job, with black upholstery and blackwall tires, done sometime in the '70s.

Left, **TOM POLLARD '29 ROADSTER:** Pollard's roadster was the classic '29 A on Deuce rails. Less traditional features included a Deuce grille with three-piece louvered hood, a '27 T windshield, a molded '40 dash with sunken S-W gauges, faired door hinges, and wild flames by Barris, with lots of great Von Dutch striping. (Pat Ganahl collection)

THE ALA KART

Owned by Richard Peters of Fresno, California, with an all-chrome chassis built by him and Blackie Gegjeian, and a full-custom body in white pearl by Barris, the Ala Kart, which began life as a '29 A roadster pickup, was the first full-on all-show hot rod. It had purple and gold scallops painted under the fenders as well as on the outside, and it had tuck-and-roll upholstery under the chassis as well as on the top and in the interior and bed. This car was not made to be driven.

It was the first roadster to win the giant AMBR trophy at Oakland twice (1958 and 1959), and it was the first real rod made into a plastic model, a hugely successful two-in-one kit by AMT.

After its extraordinary, though short, show career it suffered a couple of fires and a very long seclusion before being delivered to Roy Brizio's rod shop recently for an awaited full restoration.

ED ROTH'S BEATNIK BANDIT

When Ed Roth's free-form, fiberglass-bodied Outlaw debuted in 1960, it was the first in a decade's worth of zany, utterly unmatched "rods" from Big Daddy that have never been equaled before or since.

However, the bubble-topped 1961 Beatnik Bandit was the epitome, and arguably the best, Rothmobile of all time. He hand-shaped the body, molded it in fiberglass, painted it in pearl and candy, blew the plexiglass bubble, and set it on a much-shortened 1950 Olds chassis, complete with all-chrome, supercharged engine. The big stick inside was the accelerator, brakes, and hydraulic steering. And, while it was not practical to drive on the street, everything on it was fully operable. Roth would fire the engine regularly at shows to draw customers to his shirt-painting booth. Plastic model kits of this car still sell today.

TOM MCMULLEN'S ROADSTER

It's hard to realize today the impact Tom McMullen's car had when it appeared on *Hot Rod*'s cover in 1963. There weren't many rods on the streets, at all, during this period, let alone any with blazing flames, mag wheels, and a real, working supercharged engine and racing Moon fuel tank. And none of this was for show. McMullen regularly raced this thing on the street and strips, as well as at El Mirage. Though painted

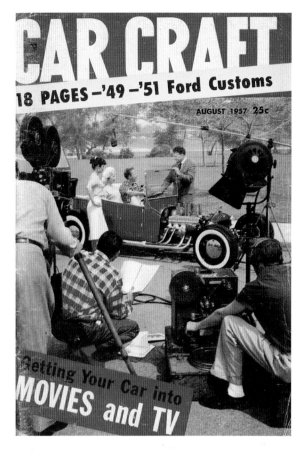

by Tom, the wild flames were laid out by Ed Roth, who also added the exuberant striping.

After retiring this highly successful car in the late '60s, Tom built two or three more-or-less close duplicates into the '90s, before his untimely death. The actual car was restored by Roy Brizio in 2003.

DOYLE GAMMEL'S COUPE

Though it was never on a magazine cover nor shown in color, Doyle Gammel's chocolate brown, chopped, full-fendered '32 three-window became an icon for later chopped Deuce coupes, spawning a frenzy for them in the mid-'70s that persists today. With its Moon tank, polished five-spoke mags, four-speed, and Corvette fuel-injected engine, it was sort of the coupe equivalent to McMullen's car when it appeared in *Rod & Custom* in '63. With black button-tufted upholstery and slicks slightly protruding from the rear fenders, it epitomizes the '60s-era rod.

After a recent, well-publicized stint in purple paint, wild flames, and white tuck-and-roll, it was acquired by collector Bruce Meyer, and is being restored by Bob Bauder.

Left, **RICHARD PE-TERS' ALA KART** Peters' Ala Kart was a show machine and not meant to be driven. It appeared parked in the gang's garage with baby-faced teen idol John Ashley in 1958's *Hot Rod Gang*. When full-custom show rods like this hit the scene in the later '50s, street-driven rods and customs faded away. The engine was an impractical fuel-injected Dodge Hemi.

Bottom, left, **ED ROTH'S BEATNIK BANDIT:** This was a love-it-or-hate-it hot rod, but the vast majority of Roth's fans, mostly young teens, loved it to death and clamored for the model, his monster shirts, and any other products he produced. (Pat Ganahl collection)

Bottom, right, **DOYLE GAMMEL COUPE:** How much you chop a top makes a big difference. Most rodders agree that three-windows look best chopped—as opposed to five-windows—and that Gammel's was perfection on wheels. (Pat Ganahl collection)

THE *AMERICAN GRAFFITI* COUPE

Nobody dreamed how successful—or enduring—George Lucas' 1973 film *American Graffiti* would be. And nobody guessed at the impact it would ultimately have during that decade on the revival of traditional hot rods and custom cars. Though most of the film's young actors went on to huge careers, most rodders agree the cars were the stars, especially John Milner's chopped yellow Deuce coupe.

Though it was in most ways a typical movie prop—the chopped grille and bobbed fenders didn't fit '62, or any other, rod style—it sure made a strong impression on the big screen, especially in motion under the night lights.

The actual car has been owned by Rick Figari of San Francisco for several years. Figari keeps it in original movie condition, and has been showing it on a national rod run circuit of late.

PETE CHAPOURIS' THE CALIFORNIA KID

When Pete Chapouris built his chopped, full-fendered, flamed, and traditional three-window '34 coupe, he had no intention of its being a movie star—he was just building one bad-ass hot rod. That's why *Rod & Custom* picked it, along with Jim Jacobs' yellow, fenderless version, for its classic barnyard November '73 cover (to tout the re-emergence of chopped hot rod coupes, influenced in no small way by Doyle Gammel's earlier version). It was only later that some Hollywood-type cast it in the Martin Sheen TV movie *The California Kid* and painted the name on the door. The extra exposure didn't hurt, but this is one Top 20 rod in its own right.

That cover meeting eventually led to Pete & Jake's well-known hot rod parts company, a legacy that Chapouris continues today with his So-Cal Speed Shop rods-and-parts emporium.

TOM PRUFER'S '34 COUPE

This car is often called the Cop Shop Coupe because it was patterned after a cartoon drawn by Dave Bell for a column heading of that name in *Street Rodder* magazine. But that's a silly name for one of the most right-on hot rods ever built. A collaboration of chassis fabricator Pete Eastwood, metal-benders Ron Covell and Dave Urehara, and custom painter and builder Rod Powell, this was the first rod (as far as we know) cut and reshaped to look like a cartoon drawing that was never intended to be built in real life.

You couldn't do much more to an early Ford to make it a real hot rod—the rake, the chop, the wheels and tires, the louvers, the nerfs, right down to the "No Club" plaque and quick-change rear end. I liked it fine when it debuted at the Oakland Show all in black in 1982. But then flame-master Rod Powell lit it on fire to complete the deal.

VERN LUCE'S COUPE

This car actually slightly predates Tom Prufer's and, though both are surprisingly similar in shape, stance, and body modification, this one quickly and thoroughly eradicated the traditional rod cues Tom's

TOM MCMULLEN'S ROADSTER: An early L.A. roadsters member, McMullen drove this car long and hard enough to go through at least two paint and upholstery jobs, not to mention engines. It was hardly ever shown or trailered. (Pat Ganahl collection)

Facing page, **THE AMERICAN GRAFFITI COUPE** The Graffiti five-window, was by no means an outstanding car in looks or craftsmanship. But its impact on the public, as a hot rod, is immeasurable. Rick Figari, from San Francisco, has been the owner of the coupe for nearly twenty years. (Photograph © David Fetherston)

Clockwise from top left, **VERN LUCE'S COUPE:** Luce's all-red coupe launched an armada of slick rods. An identical roadster version the following year won the big Oakland trophy and wore the first set of Boyd's custom-whittled billet aluminum-alloy wheels. (Pat Ganahl collection)

PETE CHAPOURIS' THE CALIFORNIA KID: The original Pete Chapouris '34 coupe was a '60s-style rod with polished Halibrand mags and no name on the door, as seen on the cover of the November 1973 issue of *Rod & Custom*. (Pat Ganahl collection)

TOM PRUFER'S '34 COP SHOP COUPE: You can't readily see all the work that went into this caricature car to drastically alter it, but the frame was pie-cut in the middle, the body leaned forward, the grille shortened and leaned back, and the hood lengthened and reshaped. It all worked with a beautiful, mean symmetry. (Photograph © Pat Ganahl)

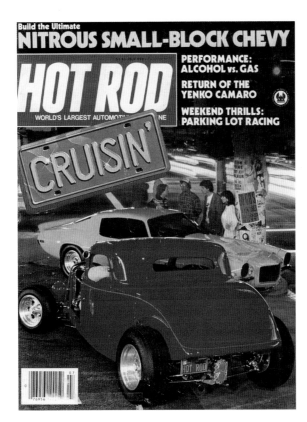

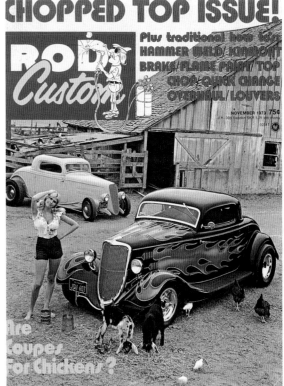

emphasized. Designed by Art Center-trained Thom Taylor and crafted in Boyd Coddington's shop, this smooth, slick coupe launched an all-new, pervasive rod trend known as "high tech" or "the billet look." Although this one, surprisingly, has vestigial door hinges, all other body "barbs" are removed—handles, louvers, or any traces of chrome trim. It rides on billet aluminum wheels with four-wheel independent suspension and disc brakes. Everything is painted red. It was a style that was certainly overdone in the '80s, but persists today, now applied to later '30s fat-fendered models.

A MONOGRAM PICTURE

with **JAMES LYDON** Art Baker · Gil Stratton, Jr. Gloria Winters · Myron Healy

Produced by JERRY THOMAS · Directed by Lewis D. Collins Screenplay by Dan Ullman

50/624

HOT ROD, 1950: This was one of the first hot rod flicks ever, and the plot would soon be repeated and recreated—with subtle revisions—in movies and on the streets for the next two decades. James Lydon was a misunderstood hot rodder who in the end triumphed at the wheel of his glorious Deuce roadster and rode off into a happy sunset.

Hot Rod Movies: *The Good, the Bad, and the Downright Silly*

They were the Automotive Age's version of the tried-and-true Western—the horse opera transformed into a hot rod ballet. It was as if Roy Rogers traded in Trigger on a T-bucket roadster or the Lone Ranger put Silver out to pasture to ride the range in a chrome-engined Deuce coupe. Born was a brave new world of mechanical steeds, and the movies were made to match.

As both the film industry and hot rodding came to life in Southern California, it's little wonder hot rods jumped to the silver screen soon after they roared onto the city streets. Local youths were yanked away from tuning engines and enlisted as stars. Hotted-up junkyard specials were turned into glamorous rides. And backroads in the undeveloped San Fernando Valley became the scenes of showdowns.

Hot rod flicks often followed westerns in their plots as well as popularity. The storylines were bare bones: there was the simple triangle of a good guy, a bad guy, and a girl. The conflict—whether it was the need to raise money for a new dragster or to battle the lawless baddie's slight—was usually settled with a duel.

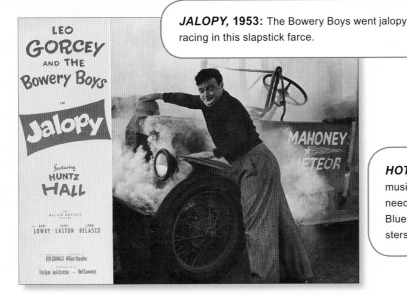

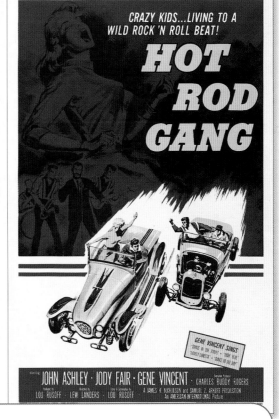

Instead of a gunfight at high noon on Main Street, the hot rodders ran a chicken race on a mountain road until the bad guy lost control and crashed into eternity.

Like the westerns, most hot rod movies were simple morality tales. There were run-ins with the law, run-ins with the older generation that didn't get the need for speed, and run-ins with bad guys in hot rods suitably painted black. In 1947's *The Devil on Wheels,* reckless hot rodders learned their lessons about driving too fast. In 1956's *Hot Rod Girl,* good and bad guy alike discover drag racing is safe only on an association-approved dragstrip. In 1958's *Hot Rod Gang,* stealing cars for parts is proven a no-no. The morals were straight out of Sunday school—with a taste of driver's ed thrown in for good measure.

The Devil on Wheels may have been the grandfather of all hot rod flicks. The teenagers build a rod, find true love, and go drag racing, setting the basic plot outline for the traffic congestion to come. The film also featured one hot-rodder's immortal words, "What's the use of hopping up a car if you can't give her the gun?" It was the hot rodder's metaphysical Big

Howco International
presents

CHARLES
COURTNEY

MELINDA
BYRON

ROBERT
FULLER

WITH THE BALLAD
TEEN AGE KISSES
SUNG BY
David Houston

TEEN AGE THUNDER

Music by Walter Greene • Screenplay by Rudy Makoul • Directed by Paul Helmick • A Marquette Production

TEEN AGE THUNDER, 1957: Like many a rod exploitation flick, *Teen Age Thunder* was basically a Western hotted-up for a new era and audience, with misunderstood teenagers wearing the black and white hats and hot rods as the high-horsepower steeds.

Question posed to the world from the big screen.

Many of the best of the bad movies featured hot music in concert with the open headers. In *Hot Rod Girl,* the first car flick to marry music with the exhaust note, the gang snaps their fingers to bebop. Just two years later in *Hot Rod Gang,* Gene Vincent and the Blue Caps rock the sock-hop. And it only got louder and faster from then on.

The classic 1950s and early 1960s hot rod and racing flicks evolved into a new generation of outcast movies in the mid-1960s and in the 1970s. The cars were now hot rods on steroids—factory-built muscle cars—and the drivers were confused anti-heroes, not knowing if they should wear a white or black hat. Frankie Avalon and Annette Funicello's 1964 *Bikini Beach Party* had given way to the sound and fury of

1971's *Two-Lane Blacktop* and 1974's *Dirty Mary, Crazy Larry.*

At the same time, nostalgia was born in 1973 with *American Graffiti,* a rose-hued look back at the way things were with hot rods, drive-ins, and good old rock and roll. Suddenly, there was a drag race to get back to the fifties.

Since then, most hot rod flicks have followed one of these two routes down the divided highway—an ode to the hot rod outlaw or a dose of hot rod nostalgia. And sometimes even these white lines get blurred with revivals of classic outlaw movies, as in 2000's *Gone in 60 Seconds* and 2001's *The Fast and the Furious.*

Through it all, one thing remains true. The cars are the stars.—Michael Dregni

HOT-ROD GIRL, 1956: Street racing, chicken races, rock and roll, and death—*Hot-Rod Girl* had them all, but the acting and plot was pure dullsville.

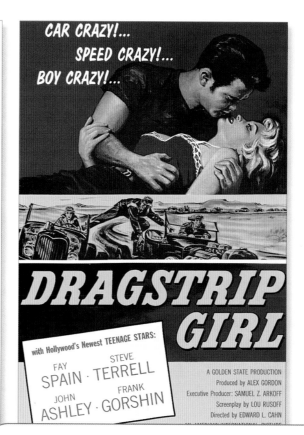

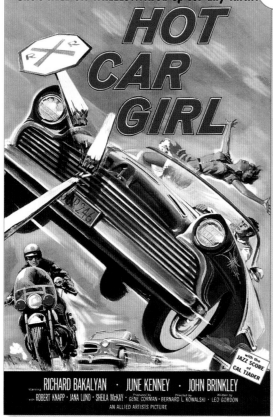

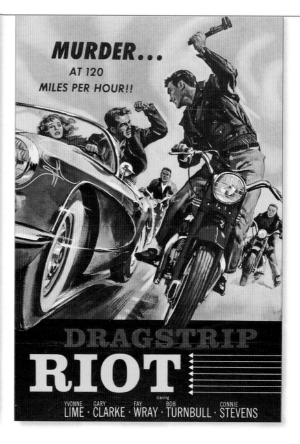

CAR CRAZY FILMS: Clockwise from top left: *Speed Crazy,* 1959; *Dragstrip Girl,* 1956; *Dragstrip Riot,* 1958; and *Hot Car Girl,* 1958.

HOT ROD RUMBLE, 1957 One-sheet poster and lobby cards showing the key moments of *Hot Rod Rumble,* one of the best of the early rodding flicks. Anti-hero Big Arnie suffers abuses from his girl, his best friend, and the hot rod gang, but overcomes all odds to win the big race—and win back his girl.

MOB RULE IN A HIG

C
...HE HAD MO

SHE TURNED A COOL-SCHOO
INTO A HOT-BED OF VIOLENC

Hear "HIGH SCHOOL CAESAR" as sung by RE

starring

JOHN ASHLEY · GARY VINSON · LOWELL BROWN · STEVE STEVEN

PRODUCED and DIRECTED BY O'DALE IRELAND · ORIGINAL STORY BY O'DALE IRELAND · ETHELMAE PAGE · RO

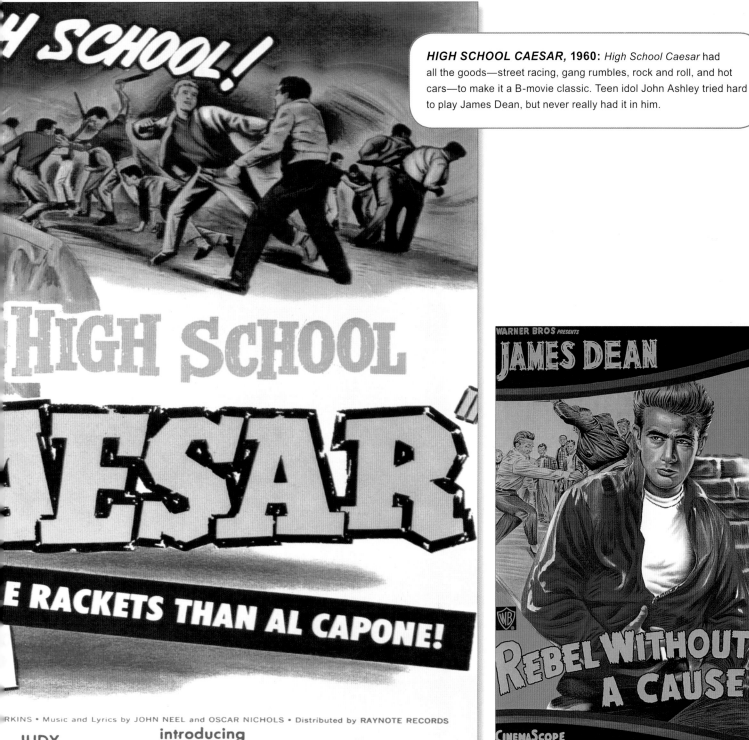

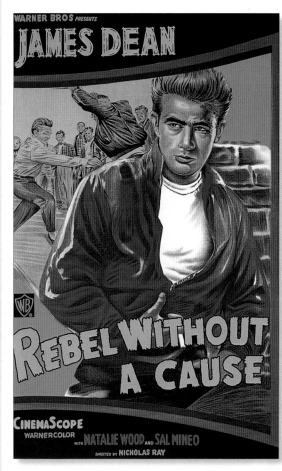

HIGH SCHOOL CAESAR, 1960: *High School Caesar* had all the goods—street racing, gang rumbles, rock and roll, and hot cars—to make it a B-movie classic. Teen idol John Ashley tried hard to play James Dean, but never really had it in him.

REBEL WITHOUT A CAUSE, 1955 Cars played a secondary role to the characters, but in the end, *Rebel without a Cause* was probably the most influential hot rod movie of all time. Chicken races, switchblade duels, loud music, and a healthy dose of angst all combined to define hot rodding culture—right or wrong—in many folks' minds. James Dean's chopped '49 Merc also set a style for cool for decades to come.

CHAPTER 3

VELOCITY

"He's a speed addict. And it's worse than dope."

—Edward De Roo, *Go, Man, Go!* 1959

SHOT ROD: Speed often came before brakes in the pioneering days of hot rodding. Many cars in the pre–World War II era didn't boast paint, chrome—or safety features. And some were even downright dangerous, earning them the moniker "shot rods." This channeled A-V8 probably looks rattier than it was, because, like most, it was still a work in progress. (Pat Ganahl collection)

From the Dry Lakes **to the Salt:**
HOT RODS AND CUSTOMS,
the Dysfunctional Siblings

By Don Pennington

Don Pennington was raised in the 1950s car culture of the California hot rod. His first car was a '50 Chev coupe, followed later by a new 1960 Chevrolet purchased from the C. S. Mead dealership of Pasadena, tuned by Don Nicholson, and raced extensively at Lions, Fontana, and Colton drag strips. In 1964, Don rented space at Evans Speed Equipment in South El Monte and campaigned a Junior Fuel dragster. Since then, he has owned a wide variety of cars, from stockers to fuelers and including many hot rods.

Working in the sign industry for years, he honed his skills as a commercial automotive artist, which later included developing and manufacturing products for the aviation and street rod industries. He began writing about cars with a column in the Pasadena High School newspaper. He currently writes the "Kickin' Rocks" column in the *Goodguys Gazette* and for other publications he writes *Karbux,* which studies collector car investment.

He currently owns a historic custom 1956 Chevrolet and crews on the renowned Geisler–Vail–Banks 1953 land-speed record-holding Studebaker.

HEART AND SOUL:
Classic Hi-Boy roadsters like Dennis Kyle's '32 Ford are the heart and soul of hot rodding. Seen sitting here in the setting sun on the Bonneville Salt Flats, its clean, stylish lines are crisp and tight, with its orange paintwork set off with fine black-and-white scallops and matching pinstriping. Its body-colored frame, chopped windshield, and Buick brakes are all part of its classic rod styling. Rolling on sixties-style American five-spokes, it's powered by a 292 Chevrolet small-block. This roadster is no slouch either, with 13-second ETs on the dragstrip. (Photograph © David Fetherston)

Walking onto the parched hardness of the dry lake beds above Los Angeles is a step into times past. Muroc, El Mirage, Rosamond, and Harper dry lakes hold a special place in the soul of anyone who appreciates hot rodding. This is where it all began. Through the twenties and thirties, souped-up cars sped across these lake beds, laying the foundation for a remarkable time in automotive history. Standing in this dusty expanse, the ghostly figures of those early years slowly reappear as if in a mirage, revealing the cars, the people, and the legends.

The genesis of these cars goes back to the twenties, when the youth of the day thought that something better could be done with the stodgy old automobiles driving around the brick streets of Los Angeles. The prime candidates for these "soup jobs" were usually Model T Fords as they were plentiful and inexpensive, but just about any roadster would do. Engines were hopped up. Fenders and windshields were cast aside to lighten and streamline the cars to better resemble the circle track racers of the day. Everything was done with one aim—to make them go faster. When modifications were complete, they had to be tested;

in the eyes of the car owners, the city streets were the logical place. As street racing became more widespread, pressure from local police grew, gradually pushing the racing to the dry lakes as this expansive tabletop of hard dirt was the perfect place to drive fast. Almost as soon as the first two cars arrived, the competitive instinct surfaced and dry lakes racing began in earnest. Hot rodding was born.

By the mid-1930s, two branches of hot rods were evolving. Some folk were racing open roadsters on the lakes—the true hot rods—while others were customizing their cars for the city streets. These personalized automobiles built for style instead of speed soon became known simply as "customs." Most customs were closed-bodied cars—coupes and sedans—which early racing rules did not allow to compete with the roadsters and handbuilt streamliners on the lake beds. And although most people liked both hot rods and customs, and many people owned both, a separation in the two styles developed that persists today.

In 1937, the Southern California Timing Association was formed, replacing the racing sanctioned

by individual clubs. During World War II, the lakes were quiet, but when the veterans returned home their pent-up desires were released by driving their hot rods back onto the lake beds. Yet the SCTA's rules expressly sequestered closed cars from racing. Bruce Geisler, a longtime dry lakes and Bonneville racer and multi-time SCTA president, remembers a rival organization, the Russetta Timing Association, which formed to include the banned coupes and sedans. His club, the Rod Riders, was a member of Russetta and had some thirty-five cars running at the lakes on a regular basis. But Russetta was starting to fold, and soon the Rod Riders began talking about moving to the SCTA. Shortly after the Rod Riders swapped associations, Russetta ceased operation. Now, officially the rod-versus-custom distinction was gone, but the two camps remained separate, albeit together under one organization. This distinction was highlighted by the title given to the startup 1950s magazine *Rod & Custom.*

When the earliest customs hit the streets, the definition of a custom was pretty clear. They were cruisers, cars for which looks were more important than performance. There were of course customs with souped-up engines, but these were in the minority. Defining a hot rod, on the other hand, was a simpler task: if a car was cut-down—with windshield, fender, and headlights removed—and went fast, it was a hot rod. "Cut-downs" or "soup jobs" were always roadsters. Yet as these cars gradually changed with time, a bone of contention began to develop as to who had a hot rod and who didn't. Over the years the hard-core hot rodders believed that hot rods didn't have fenders. Hot rods were and are performance machines, and in the last couple of decades, the owners of cars with hot engines have been calling themselves hot rodders and their cars hot rods, no matter if their car is a roadster or coupe. Even a later-model four-door sedan with fenders can be included or excluded from the hot rod fraternity simply by its tailpipe note. The line drawn in the sand defining hot rods has blurred considerably over time.

PURE RAT ROD: This classic five-window primer rod is pure rat rod. As one Shifters club member says, "We're a down-to-basics car club, we drive our cars no matter what the weather 'cause that's all we have. People say they see more of the Shifters on the side of the freeway than at the car shows but, for us, that's a great compliment. The old-time hot rodders say they used to do the same thing forty years ago!" (Photograph © David Fetherston)

Although hot rods and customs were visually different, their owners were often the same people. Bruce Geisler, who has been around over the last fifty years, enjoys and owns both hot rods and customs. His passion for cars started during the early '50s and his high school years in Montebello, California, when he was driving a new 1953 Ford convertible with Oldsmobile power and he formed one of Los Angeles' earliest clubs, the Chipmunks Car Club. His interest in cars extended into the daily activities of his father's business, Geisler Construction, which built the Fontana Drag Strip in Southern California. Geisler Construction also soon became the sponsor of Bruce's early race cars. Yet despite this shared interest, the rod and custom camps have remained subtly separated.

Through the 1930s and 1940s, racing flourished on the dry lakes. As speeds increased so did the need for a longer racing venues. Top-speed racing had been taking place for years on the Bonneville Salt Flats, a hundred miles west of Salt Lake City. Wally Parks, founder and longtime head man at the National Hot Rod Association, and Robert Petersen, founder of *Hot Rod Magazine*, pursued the idea of having a national hot rod speed trial there. Soon, they acquired a permit to have a "test event" there in the summer of 1949. Since that time, the Mecca of hot rodding has been unofficially located on those salt flats.

Bonneville 1959 saw the arrival of the Chipmunks Car Club's '29 Ford roadster with Bruce at the wheel. By year's end, the Chipmunks' roadster was due for a rebuild to make it more show-worthy and maybe faster—the show and the go, the hot rodder and the custom guy were still alive and well. Bruce disassembled the car, but as the next racing season approached he knew the roadster would not be ready. The search began for a temporary replacement.

Bruce's new car perfectly personified the dichotomy between the hot rod and custom fraternity. The car was a coupe with fenders, yet it was pure go. You couldn't exactly label it either a custom or a rod, which was fine by Bruce. His new machine was a Studebaker, which was a bit of an anomaly itself in the hot rod world. The injected Chevrolet small-block and trans from Bruce's old roadster went into

BONNEVILLE ROD:
Tom and Diana Branch's channeled '32 roadster is a classic rod of the first order. Powered by a '63 Studebaker V8, its 6-inch channel job put it low and lean to the ground, while its bare metal bodywork creates a distinctive look—especially with the gold and silver '55 Studebaker hubcaps. Its neat Mexican Serape blanket interior is also classic early hot rod trimming. Seen here on Bonneville Salt Flats during Speed Week, it was a perfect slice of the hot rod pie. (Photograph © David Fetherston)

15th ANNUAL
BONNEVILLE
NATIONAL SPEED TRIALS
BONNEVILLE SALT FLATS -- WENDOVER, UTAH
SUN. AUG. 18 THRU SAT. AUG. 24

72 COMPETITION CLASSES
TROPHIES FOR ALL CLASSES AND RECORDS

OFFICIAL PROGRAM

BONNEVILLE '68

20th ANNIVERSARY

75¢

TWENTIETH ANNUAL
NATIONAL SPEED TRIALS

BONNEVILLE

1960

The world's fastest racing course
Tooele County, Utah

BONNEVILLE SALT FLATS
'59

the world's fastest racing course
Tooele County, Utah

THIS CAR HAS PASSED THE SAFETY AND TECHNICAL INSPECTION

1958 — THE WORLD'S SAFEST SPEED EVENT — BONNEVILLE NATIONALS SAFETY INSPECTION

PARTICIPANT
TENTH ANNUAL
BONNEVILLE NATIONAL
SPEED TRIALS
Sponsored by
Southern California Timing Assn.
AUGUST 25 thru 31
1958

BONNEVILLE HOP UP MAGAZINE 1951

97 F/C
OVER 100 MPH

88 PLASTIC DYNAMICS
OVER 200 MPH

147 B
OVER 300 MPH

1 9 6 3   1 9 6 3

Presented by Southern California Timing Association, Inc.

FOR INFORMATION OR
ENTRY BLANKS, WRITE:
BONNEVILLE NATIONALS, INC.
9607 PONCIANA ST., PICO RIVERA, CALIF.

BONNEVILLE MEMORABILIA

BONNEVILLE NATIONAL SPEED TRIALS

★ 1958 ★

FIFTY CENTS

First Annual
BONNEVILLE NATIONAL SPEED TRIALS
PRESENTED BY SOUTHERN CALIFORNIA TIMING ASSOCIATION

1 9 4 9

THESE STRAIGHTAWAY SPEED TRIALS, CONDUCTED ON THE SMOOTH SURFACE OF THE BONNEVILLE SALT FLATS LOCATED NEAR WENDOVER, UTAH, ARE PRESENTED IN THE INTEREST OF FURTHERING THE DEVELOPMENT OF AMATEUR AUTOMOBILE TESTING INTO A RECOGNIZED AND ACCEPTED AMERICAN SPORT.

25¢

August 22nd to 27th

SOUVENIR PROGRAM

SECOND ANNUAL
BONNEVILLE NATIONAL SPEED TRIALS

Conducted annually, these straightaway speed trials are presented in the interest of furthering the development and recognition of amateur automotive experimentation as a beneficial and educational sport.

25¢ AUGUST 21-27 1950

THIRD ANNUAL *Bonneville*
NATIONAL SPEED TRIALS
PRESENTED BY SOUTHERN CALIFORNIA TIMING ASSOCIATION

August 27th to September 2nd 1951

SOUVENIR PROGRAM 25¢

BONNEVILLE NATIONAL SPEED TRIALS

AUGUST 25-31, 1952
(BONNEVILLE, UTAH, SALT FLATS)
CO-SPONSORED BY
SOUTHERN CALIFORNIA TIMING ASSOCIATION
AND
HOT ROD MAGAZINE

SOUVENIR PROGRAM

"World's Safest Automotive Speed Trials"

6th ANNUAL
Bonneville
NATIONAL SPEED TRIALS

10TH ANNIVERSARY

FIFTH ANNUAL
Bonneville
NATIONAL SPEED TRIALS

"world's safest automotive speed trials"

SOUVENIR PROGRAM 25¢

1955

7th ANNUAL
Bonneville
NATIONAL SPEED TRIALS

SOUVENIR PROGRAM
8th ANNUAL
BONNEVILLE
NATIONAL SPEED TRIALS

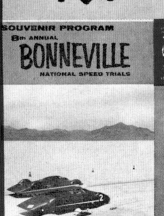

SOUVENIR PROGRAM
9th ANNUAL 1957
BONNEVILLE
NATIONAL SPEED TRIALS

35¢

1 9 5 6

BONNEVILLE NATIONAL
SPEED TRIALS
★
1 9 5 8

10TH ANNIVERSARY

the Stude for its first race at El Mirage in early 1960. The roadster would now never be completed as the number 219 Stude became Bruce's focus; after doing a lot of chrome work, Bruce sold the roadster and it was eventually parted out. A few months following the acquisition of the Stude, Bruce also picked up a Corvette as a daily driver—it too soon was also being raced, eventually setting numerous records.

Bruce's Stude has raced for more than forty years at Bonneville, set fifty records, and has boasted numerous partnerships with the likes of Gary Vail, Gale Banks, Mike Cook, Bob Kehoe, and Don Stringfellow. The relationships that have developed over those years are a Who's Who of the speed industry. When Doug Thorley had a muffler shop in East Los Angeles and needed a pit dug, it was Bruce that loaned him the equipment to do the job. A Doug's Headers logo is still on the side of the Stude today, and at a NHRA Hall of Fame induction, Doug stood up for Bruce.

In the early sixties, Bruce and Gale Banks were both running Studebakers and soon they decided to share shop space, from which they ran the two cars. To appreciate the next event you must understand that Bruce is not an unkempt person, but his attention to detail is noticeably more casual than Gale's, who likes things tidily put in their place. Apparently their shop had been a redwood furniture factory, so every time you closed the door a new cloud of dust would drift down from the rafters. Although Bruce is not afraid of a broom, he clearly has First Empty Space syndrome, meaning that when you have something in your hand, the first empty space you see is where it belongs. We are not sure if it was this or the redwood dust, but soon the Bruce and Gale Show made different turns at the corner. They remain lasting friends, but under separate roofs.

Decades later, Gale's operations spearheaded the S-15 Bonneville pickup truck for GMC and a Firebird for Pontiac that would include Bruce. Today, when Bruce visits the impossibly busy Mr. Turbo Banks at his complex in Azusa, California, special considerations are in order. During a recent visit with several friends in tow, it was clear that Gale had a full plate that day, as he was locked in his office.

Shortly after Bruce began beating on his door, Gale personally gave a grand tour of his facility to the group. Friendships such as these seem to be routine in Bruce's garage.

Through the years, Bruce's Stude has used numerous Chevrolet engines and one Buick from 258 to 383 cubic inches. One of the most powerful was a small-block Chevrolet from Banks' shop; it displaced 304 cubic inches with twin turbos pushing the car to a 209-mph record in 1980. This engine also made a one-way pass of 242 mph in 1978, only to blow a tire on a subsequent record run, nearly destroying the car. In 1981 and again in 1984, the car made several mid-220-mph passes. Bruce's ongoing interest in customs surfaced on the Stude when he attempted to run fender skirts at Bonneville, claiming they were factory options for the car. It didn't work. These experiences, friendships, records, and many awards have established Bruce Geisler as a cornerstone hot rodder and custom car enthusiast.

If at any time during the past fifty years you searched out groups interested only in hot rods or customs, you would have certainly found them. In either group there would be strong feelings about their particular interests and negative viewpoints concerning the other. At the same time, you would find people like Bruce Geisler who are recognized as stalwart hot rodders or custom guys but who also enjoy and appreciate the other. This separation has never been officially established or promoted by any sanctioning body since those early years; it just happened—hot rodders ran with hot rodders and the customs were cruising together.

Today, the separation seems stronger than ever. Traditional hot rodding and the perpetuation of dry lakes and Bonneville racing have refocused the original hot rod spirit. The insurgence of import cars that enjoy performance and customizing at the same time has likewise revitalized the custom-look cars. Taking a broad view of the auto enthusiast's world, it may appear much different than in the early days, but a closer look past the cars themselves reveals that the motivation of the owners—be they hot rodders or customizers—is unchanged. The love of cars, hot rod or custom, is shared by all.

Facing page, **CONTENDER:** This chopped and black-flamed '40 Ford coupe has long been a land speed record contender at Bonneville Speed Week. First modified for land speed racing back in the 1950s by the Boyd brothers of Oregon, it turned as fast as 120 mph during the 1990s in the care of owners Jerry and Karel Helwig. Powered by a 270 fuel-injected Flathead V8, this glorious rod racer features classic Moon discs and fuel tank. (Photograph © David Fetherston)

My Memories of BONNEVILLE Are All **A BLUR**

By Gale Banks

To most car buffs, Gale Banks' name is synonymous with turbochargers. But Banks is known for many aspects of high-performance engineering; his contribution to the Buick Grand National, GMC Syclone pickup, and 800-hp twin-turbo Chevy Camaro Limited Edition vehicles; and numerous land speed records. At heart, he's a simple hot rodder.

Gale credits the growth of his business, Gale Banks Engineering, to a childhood fascination with speed. After-school evenings were spent in his dad's garage learning everything he could about engines. At the age of sixteen, Gale was first hired to custom-build a high-performance engine. Now, several decades later, he hasn't stopped.

Banks Engineering owns the current records for World's Fastest Pickup Truck and World's Fastest Piston-Engine Automobile. For ten years, Gale held the unbroken record for World's Fastest Passenger Car—an 1,800-hp twin-turbo Firebird that blistered the Bonneville Salt Flats in 1987 and took the championship. This "stock-body door-slammer with optional tilt-wheel, power windows and AM-FM with cassette" ran 287 mph—burning nothing but straight gasoline.

In this essay, Gale looks back on what keeps him coming back to the Salt.

Facing page, **COME ONE, COME ALL:** A colorful poster advertising the 1987 Bonneville Speed Week.

Following pages, **BACK TO MUROC:** California's Muroc Dry Lake was once home to hot rods. Nowadays it's part of Edwards Air Force Base and one of the landing sites for the space shuttle—which seems like a perfectly fitting progression. In the 1990s, after a hiatus of some fifty years, hot rods were invited back to Muroc for a reunion of speed runs. Jake Jacobs' yellow coupe was parked here among a cadre of other spectators. (Photograph © Pat Ganahl)

From the official program of the 49th Annual Bonneville Speed Week 1997: "Before there was drag racing . . . Before there was NASCAR . . . Before there was off-road, Baja, SODA, SCORE . . . Before there was road racing, IMSA, Trans-AM, Formula One, FIA . . . Before there were Indy cars, sprinters, midgets, hobby stocks, rally cars, Pikes Peak, Destruction Derby and the World of Outlaws. Before there were Mears, Unsers, Andrettis, Foyt and Barney Oldfield. Even before Wally Parks . . . There was Speed."

Testing top speed started with the first automobile, and I'm willing to bet, the second automobile was intended to beat the first. Even the most uninitiated person holds an opinion about speed. Stop anywhere while towing your racer and somebody is bound to ask, "How fast will that thing go?"

Hot rodders have been answering the "how fast" question on various California dry lakes since before World War II. During the early years, Bonneville was basically a rich man's playground, where monster land speed cars ran under the old AAA sanctioning, while the dry-lakes hot rodders looked on with envy.

Enter the Southern California Timing Association (SCTA). They wanted to run "hot rods" at the Salt. A recent letter from Wally Parks explains what took place.

Dear Gale:

Alex Xydias told me you're having some difficulty unraveling the history of hot rod cars running at the Bonneville Salt Flats. Here, right from the old horse's mouth, are some details of the history of hot rod cars running at the Bonneville Salt Flats:

In 1948, when I was secretary and general manager of the SCTA as its first full-time employee, we had contacted the old AAA regarding the hope we might run our cars on the Salt. In a reply letter from Mr. Art Pillsbury, then the AAA's chief steward for auto racing in the United States, we were advised that "the world record in Class C is 203 mph and it is highly doubtful any hot rod will ever attain that speed."

Some time after that not-encouraging response, I contacted the Salt Lake City Chamber of Commerce, whose secretary, Gus Backman, was in charge of its

Bonneville Speedway Association—entrusted by the state and U.S. government as the official custodian of Bonneville's Salt Flats.

Mr. Backman suggested a meeting to discuss the SCTA's proposal, and I invited Mr. Lee Ryan, senior member of a publicity group with whom we were planning SCTA's first Hot Rod Exposition, to accompany me to the Salt Lake City presentation. As neither of us had transportation suitable for the journey, we invited Bob "Pete" Petersen to join us on the trip with his 10-year-old Mercury club coupe as our hopeful round-trip conveyance.

After our proposal, in which Lee Ryan added a valuable element of maturity, Mr. Backman agreed to allow the SCTA one "trial" event on the Bonneville Salt Flats, with any future consideration pending the first event's outcome. Needless to say, the initial venture in 1949 was a pronounced success. And due to SCTA's diligence in operations, plus the cooperative support of Union Oil Company and Hot Rod Magazine, the Bonneville National Speed Trials became a historic annual occasion—one that has lasted for half a century—threatened only by the condition of the Salt.

Wally Parks

Named in the 1949 entries were enough heroes to last me a lifetime. Today, Speed Week is the crown jewel in what has become a summer of time trials. And Bonneville, the Mecca of Speed.

While the story here is "fast," it's the people—what they build and bring to race—that makes this place so incredibly interesting. Bonneville is about dreams—and sometimes even fantasies—brought to life after months or even years of effort, and towed to this place each year with only one thing in mind: Speed.

Stirred by Bob Petersen's *Hot Rod Magazine*, I started hot rodding in 1954 by building a B-blocked, C-cranked, and Riley-headed '31 Ford Model A. But it was my '53 Stude coupe and a guy named Bruce Geisler that got me to the Salt, and neither of us has been the same since. By the way, my first run at the Salt was 150.00 mph, a perfection I have yet to duplicate.

After the run, I checked the valve lash on my 327 Chevy. Two intake rockers were clear off the studs. So much for those trick rocker nuts. To my knowledge, that was the first run by a 90-degree Chevy V-6 at the Salt.

One run. Then it rained, and we all went home to return the next year. Ah, Bonneville . . .

My business turned to turbocharging and marine engines in the '60s and '70s, but we always had our hand in something "salty." One of the most bizarre projects belonged to (then Air Force doctor) Al Abbott, who wanted to purchase one of our big-block marine endurance engines. His intent was to set the Bicycle Land Speed Record!

Turns out, he was doing this while drafting a '55 Chevy coupe. But during practice runs his engine kept kicking out parts with Al in its wake. Our boat-motor solved the problem, and Al got the record, cycling somewhere in the 145 mph range. Al's brother sat in the trunk observing and running the throttle, with another guy up front doing the steering and shifting.

Like I said, the story is the people.

And the people can be very special. In 1981, the Sundowner Corvette brought giant smiles to the faces of Bob Kehoe and myself by giving partner Dwayne McKinney a 240+ mph ride. We broke the record a ton, and proceeded to celebrate in a friend's motorhome with the blender at full rpm. We neglected the valve work needed on our engine in Geisler's Hanky Panky Studebaker. Near the end of the day, Doug Cook knocks on the door to say, "Hey Gale, I finished the heads for the Stude." Hell, I'd forgotten all about them. Doug had his own stuff to work on, but that's Bonneville . . . I'll never forget it. Today, Doug's son Mike will be found prominently placed in this program.

Through the years, having raced in almost every form of car or boat, I find that my most meaningful memories come from the Salt: Dipping my jeans and T-shirt in a 55-gallon drum of borate solution (couldn't afford a fire suit). Attempting to float my '56 Bel Air tow car on the way to the highway (it sank). Watching the guy next door bore a block in his motel room (El Patio). Running a Pontiac Firebird with factory sponsorship (talk about pressure!). Taking away a Porsche world record with a GMC pickup (the Syclone). My membership in the Rod Riders with Bill Burke as president (a true gentleman who influenced me greatly). And living with the antics of my lifelong partner, Bruce Geisler (three all-nighters in a row, and still laughing).

Bonneville is the last bastion of the amateur racer and, like Doug and Mike Cook, it's family and friendly. People with big heads are rare. I've seen direct competitors loan parts and tools to each other, sometimes even helping the other guy wrench. Then they'd go out and pump Salt with the prime intent of blowing the other guy off.

Speaking of pumping Salt, you'll find no taxiing aircraft (jet cars) at Speed Week. Here, all the cars put the power down through the tires, just like God intended. The best at that for more years than I can remember is Elwin "Al" Teague. Refining his Lakester into a Streamliner and marching well into the 400s, Al typifies what Bonneville racing is all about—limited budget, hard work, racing savvy, natural engineering talent, finding more speed year after year, and laying down a sound that defines this place. This unassuming man does not like confining spaces, yet sits in a claustrophobic place and gets in the wind with an authority that is the envy of us all.

Bonneville is about hard work and heroes, high-and low-buck, victory and defeat, fathers and sons, dreams realized and "wait'll next year." But, it's this year, and you're here. If you're racing, good luck. If you're spectating, check out the machinery—the ingenuity is awesome. Pick your favorites and see how they do. Most of all, enjoy the meet, whether you're in it or along the sidelines.

People say, "In life, timing is everything." But here at Bonneville, I like to say, "Everything is timing!"

Dragging

By Roy Newton

Roy Newton was just another all-American boy bitten by the automobile bug early on in life. Like many, he dreamed of hot rods until the day when he finally could drive, built a rod of his own, and took it for that first spin. The speed felt so good, the next thing he knew he was racing on the streets, which soon led to safer racing on tracks and dragstrips.

Roy's racing tales are quintessentially American stories of machinery and speed. They have it all: the kind of boasting that built the Paul Bunyan legends; picaresque misadventures with shadetree tuning and homemade performance; and a healthy dose of humor. These are truly a remembrance of fast times past.

FLAGMAN: Alive with sudden sound and fury, a hot rod race launches.

The first race car I owned was in 1959, and this will kill you when I tell you this. You see, it was a 1937 Ford coupe, cut down, and made into a stock car. It had the front-distributor Flathead motor with just a small camshaft and a little carburetor work. The car was ready to race, and I gave the owner $50 for it.

I ran in the Sportsman class on tracks in Hialeah and Hollywood, Florida. At that time, some of the big names that were racing there were Bobby Allison, Rod Perry, Gene Winn, Roy Clanton, and Bill Hess. A couple of these names you might know, because they went on to drive NASCAR.

I had never driven a circle track or any other racetrack before, but how hard could it be? All you had to do is aim it down the straightaway and turn the corner—or at least that's how it looked. I didn't have a problem with nerve: My first time out, I drove down that straightaway as fast as I could go and turned the corner. All of a sudden I was going the wrong way. It was a real good thing it was only warmups and nobody hit me. Well, in the course of a year I hit the wall ten times, turned over once, and completely left the track on another occasion and hit a phone pole. The best I did in that first year was a third place finish.

In those days, we didn't use trailers; we pulled the cars with tow bars. My wife-to-be, her brother, and I went racing one Saturday night. It had rained that day and was a little muddy, but we went ahead and raced anyway. It was a paved track, so the wet pits didn't matter as the track was dry. I ran my normal fourth or fifth, then it was time to head home. I pulled the stock car up behind my '52 Ford and hooked up the tow bar. We all jumped in the '52, I put it in reverse, and the shift linkage fell off. We couldn't go forward as we were in a swamp. The stock car couldn't pull us out, either; it just spun its wheels. By this time everyone had left. I had to lay in 2 inches of mud to put that linkage back on with a bobbie pin. To make things worse, the car was lowered. Everyone else was having a good time, but I failed to see the humor. When I got up from the mudbath, I took my shirt and pants off, wrapped a blanket around myself, and drove home.

About two weeks later, my dad told me to hook up the race car. He worked with a part-time guard for the Hialeah track and he had gotten me an hour of practice time. While the guard and my dad sat on the wall and had a beer, I got to drive on the track all by myself. In the end, though, it didn't seem to help much. I still couldn't do better than third.

We used to race on the oval track on Saturday night, change tires, and drag race on Sunday. It was early in drag racing and we used an old World War II airfield. There was no such thing as a starting tree. We used a flagman, and the smart racers worked out signals with the flagman to get a head start. By that time, there was no catching them.

After a few years racing the '37 Ford, all the wrecks were taking their toll. The frame was so bad it was ready to turn by itself. That might have been okay if I could have run the track backwards, but the car was turning the wrong way to go forward. So I sold the running gear out of the '37 and scrapped the body. It was probably melted down and is now a Honda.

I had been building a '55 Plymouth, and when it was ready I painted it bright orange with white letters and the number 5. I wanted to make sure everyone could see me. It was powered by a 392-cubic-inch Hemi. The company I worked for would send a wrecker to the track on race night, so I no longer had to tow-bar the car. Now I was in the Big Time. I ran the '55 for a while but still the best I ever ran was third.

One Saturday night, one of the track's hot shoes drove my '55 and won. Now I knew it was not the car—it was the driver.

The car could win, but the driver needed work. The harder I tried, the more that wall took over. The car had so much power that when you came out of the corner and hit the gas, you had to feather it just right to keep from going into that wall. It only took a few years to figure out the problem. You see, I was born blind in my right eye and I could not judge the distance to the wall. In fact, I could not see it at all, so I hit it a lot. If I slowed down so I didn't hit the wall, I didn't go fast enough to win. I think the reason so few '55 Plymouths are being restored today is because I used up all the right front fenders and doors while racing.

STREET RACING ... AND SPEEDING TICKETS

Due to my problems with that wall, drag racing was looking better and better to me. All you had to do was be good on the start and go straight down the track—there were no corners or walls to hit. I put my brain in gear and formulated a plan for a fast car.

My daily ride was a '54 Ford with a 256-cubic-inch Mercury engine in it. I put what they called at the time a full-race cam in the Y-block. Back in those days, when you bought a camshaft they were listed as full-race, three-quarters-race, or light street; there were no high-tech cams available. I did many hours of work on the cylinder heads, then got what was called a log-intake manifold. You had to weld it together and it looked like two logs, one on each side and each holding three two-barrel carbs. When you got it all put together, you had a six two-barrel setup. With this much carburetion, the bottom end of the rpm range suffered a little, but after 2,000 rpm, it hauled butt.

We did a lot of street racing in those days. Police radios were not as good as they are today. There was

no eye in the sky or night vision either. The cop cars were not as fast as the hot rods and that made it easy on us. That '54 was one running chunk of iron.

One night while out cruising, I ran across another bad boy and the next thing I knew we were on our way. I'm not sure we even waited for the green. Just about the time I hit third gear, I saw the lights flashing on the cop car behind us. I went one way and the other guy went the other. I looked in the mirror and the cop was coming my way. I turned three or four really fast corners and was going as quick as I could when I pulled into a lot behind a store. I got out of the car and started walking home. The cop car must have passed by me three times. When I got home, my wife didn't even ask me where the car was; this was not the first time this had happened.

I then put a lower gear in the rear end to improve the bottom end of the rpm range. By now, I had a four-speed transmission in the car because I kept breaking the cluster gear in the three-speed. My brother-in-law and I went out to test the car on a deserted road where we had marked off a quarter mile. About halfway through third gear, we flashed past a trooper sitting on a side road. I kept going down the road, then pulled over and lifted the hood and played like I was fixing something. The trooper came flying up and stopped behind us—and boy, was he mad! He was all red in the face and asked me what in hell I was doing. I told him my gas pedal had stuck down to the floor. By now he was looking under the hood himself and asking questions about all those carbs. He was still upset and told me if he could have got his radar gun up in time, I'd be cooling my heels in jail. He checked the whole car over but everything worked, and all he could do was lecture me.

We South Florida street racers were getting away with a lot in the early days, but all that was about to come to an end—an abrupt end. My buddy had a '57 Chevy that was one of the baddest rides around, and one Friday night we went out cruising. A guy with a '61 Ford came up and wanted to prove his car was the fastest. We went to Chrone Avenue, lined up, and away we went. It was a close race, and the '57 had just hit third gear when out of nowhere came a trooper in a 426 Wedge Dodge and he pointed for us to pull over. Because ours were two of the fastest cars around, we knew that street racing was history.

I tried several other Y-block Fords—a '55 with a 312 and a '57 with a 312 fed by two four-barrel carbs. But there was one small problem called the small-block Chevy. It was taking big-block Fords to outrun a Chevrolet small-block.

Drag racing in those early days was not safe—and I mean at the dragstrip. The first tracks were old airbases without walls or stands. We used to just line up our cars alongside the quarter-mile and spectate. One Sunday, a few friends and I went to see the big boys race. There was an Austin with a fuel-injected Chev in it and that car would really haul. We were sitting about halfway down the track in front of my car; my wife Ruby was resting on a little box and I was on the fender. The Austin and a '56 Chev took

off and were about one-third down the track. All of a sudden, the front engine pulley came off the Austin. We saw it rolling across the track like a bowling ball down the lane. I grabbed Ruby and took off. The pulley hit the box and her shoes, then bowled right into the door of my car. Two weeks later a racer rolled his car; it caught fire and went into the bystanders and their cars. The driver was killed and four or five other people hurt. That was the last race on that airstrip.

Now we were back where we started with no place to race except on the street. It would be another two years before we had an honest-to-goodness real dragstrip, with starting tree and all. It cost us a little money to get in, but it was a lot cheaper than

the speeding tickets we had been getting for the past two years.

GETTING THE REAR END DOWN TO BUSINESS

Now you'd think we'd be happy with a new racetrack, but the first thing we found out was that you could not red light the old flagman, but you sure could with the starting tree. The second thing was that there was something wrong with the track. The brand new track that we loved so much slowed down all the cars. The 12- and 13-second cars slowed to 14 and 15 seconds. It didn't take us long to figure out that marking a quarter-mile on a road and timing with a stop watch just did not work. This was the point in time when we knew we either had to become racers or give it up. Out of the twelve guys that I ran with, only three of us kept going back to the track as racers.

By this time I had a '64 Pontiac Grand Prix with a 421 engine and a four-speed trans, the fastest car I had owned to this time. My GP had the power but it was hard to get it to the ground. The next thing I knew I was carrying around a set of 7-inch slicks in the trunk. The first run I made with the GP was 15.7, and I had it in my mind that I had a 13-second

MONSTER DRAG RACERS: Straight from television's *The Munsters*, Herman Munster's "Munster Koach" squares off against Gramps Munster's "Drag-U-La" coffin car. Both machines were built by George Barris in 1964.

car. It was pretty clear that all of that bench racing did not make your car fast.

The one thing I did figure out was that speed costs money. The big question was how fast did you want to go? Now we were down to just two of us guys racing, which was the way it stayed. But us two could not stop.

I got the GP down to 14.5 and realized that a 4,300-pound car was just not going to go much faster and still be drivable on the street. My brother-in-law, my nephew, and I went to the track one particular Wednesday night. I was trying different jets in the carb and changing timing to go for a better time. I had gotten the GP down to 14.1 @ 112 mph and badly wanted to be in the 13s. I let the slicks down to 7 pounds of air pressure, got to the line, had the rpms at 3,500, and popped the clutch. All of a sudden, there was a loud bam and the car lost all power. It seems that I broke an axle, and there we were 15 miles from home. I had just overhauled the Posi-Trac and happily those new clutches allowed us to drive the car home. If we had to come to a complete stop, we would have had to push the car for some time after that, and the Posi still worked. I replaced the axle and owned the car for some time after that, and the Posi continued to work. That axle has become a family legend.

I did get the GP to the 13s a couple of times. But in those days there were no ET brackets; it was all classes. The classes were rated on horsepower-to-weight, and the GP was so far off its class record that I knew I could never win class. The car was great on Wednesday's Grudge Night, but it should have been called Money Night. The car was so big looking, it wasn't hard to find guys that just knew they could outrun it. At that time, low 14s for a street car was good and I made a lot of money with that GP.

I knew if I was going to win races that meant something, I was going to have to change the way I raced. I went and got myself a '68 Pontiac GTO with 18,000 miles on it. It had a 400-cubic-inch engine with a 400 transmission and a 3.23 rear axle ratio. I checked it over, and the next Wednesday night I took it to the track to see what she would do. The very first pass with street tires, the car went 14.4 @ 99 mph. I knew with some work, this car would really go.

The first thing I did was to change the rear axle ratio to a 3.90. That is about as low as you can go and still drive the car all the time. I had already learned that if you do one thing at a time, it saves you a lot of headache in the long run trying to sort things out. The next time I went to the track, my GTO went 14.1 @ 101 mph.

Now I knew I was going to have to find some horsepower somewhere. No matter what you've heard, the muscle cars of those days didn't go better than the mid-14s to low-15s, fresh from the factory.

The second thing I did was to put a Pontiac HO camshaft in the GTO and make the valvetrain adjustable. Pontiac engines had a problem with valve float at 5,500 rpm if you did not make the valvetrain adjustable. When I went back to the track, it pulled a lot better on the top end and went 13.8 @ 106 mph.

Now it was time for the hard work—getting the timing, carb, and distributor all set up right. It also

SPEED SHOP

MOON EQUIPMENT COMPANY 10820 SO. NORWALK BLVD.
SANTA FE SPRINGS, CALIF. 90670

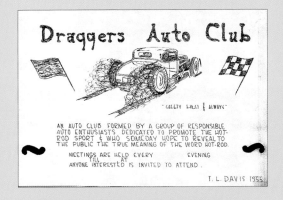

Draggers Auto Club

"SAFETY FIRST & ALWAYS"

AN AUTO CLUB FORMED BY A GROUP OF RESPONSIBLE
AUTO ENTHUSIASTS DEDICATED TO PROMOTE THE HOT-
ROD SPORT & WHO SOMEDAY HOPE TO REVEAL TO
THE PUBLIC THE TRUE MEANING OF THE WORD HOT-ROD.

MEETINGS ARE HELD EVERY   EVENING
             TILL   AT
ANYONE INTERESTED IS INVITED TO ATTEND.

T. L. DAVIS 1955

Charlestown
DRAG RACES

JULY 1
Also: August 5
October 7

Sanction

CHARLESTOWN, RHODE ISLAND
CHARLESTOWN DRAGWAY
7 Miles S.E. of Westerly on RT. 1

Mel Larson's
PHOENIX
ML
DRAG STRIP
RACE DRIVER

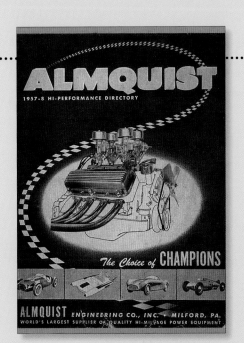

ALMQUIST
1957-8 HI-PERFORMANCE DIRECTORY

The Choice of CHAMPIONS

ALMQUIST ENGINEERING CO., INC. • MILFORD, PA.
WORLD'S LARGEST SUPPLIER OF QUALITY HI-MILEAGE POWER EQUIPMENT

DRAGWAY
42
WEST SALEM
OHIO

DRAG RACING MEMORABILIA

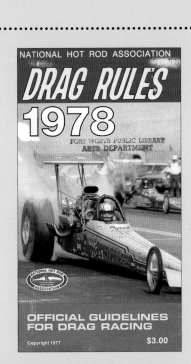

NATIONAL HOT ROD ASSOCIATION
DRAG RULES
1978

FORT WORTH PUBLIC LIBRARY
ARTS DEPARTMENT

**OFFICIAL GUIDELINES
FOR DRAG RACING**

Copyright 1977 $3.00

PHOENIX INTERNATIONAL
PARTICIPANT
PIR
115th Ave. & BASELINE RD.
RACEWAY DRAGSTRIP

OLD RT. 35, 3 MI. WEST OF XENIA, O.
KIL-KARE
DRAGSTRIP and SPEEDWAY
HOME OF THE ROAD KNIGHTS

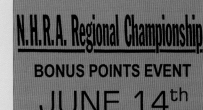

ROUTE 1, CHARLESTOWN, RHODE ISLAND

N.H.R.A. Regional Championship

BONUS POINTS EVENT
JUNE 14th

cash and merchandise awards

MAIN GATE OPENS	8 A.M.
TIME TRAILS BEGIN	9 A.M.
INSPECTION CLOSES	12 P.M.
ELIMINATIONS	1 P.M.

STRIP SPECIFICATIONS:
OVER 1 MILE LONG   250' WIDE
WELDER ON PREMISES   FULLY PAVED PIT AREA

CHARLESTOWN, RHODE ISLAND
CHARLESTOWN DRAGWAY
7 Miles S.E. of Westerly on RT. 1

would not hurt if I could get the rear end to stick to the ground.

You must remember in those days we had no computers to help us set up cars—you simply had to be a good mechanic. The next couple of weeks were spent trying to get the distributor right. It was the old point type and you could do a lot to them. I also put a timing tape on the front pulley so I could get the total timing in by 3,000 rpm. It was also time to get some slicks for the car. I was going to run stock class, so I could only use 7-inch slicks. I was still racing the '64 GP, so I had to get two spare rims and some new slicks for the GTO. I went back to the track

with the slicks, and after playing with the timing, I got 13.1 @ 110 mph.

Now don't forget I was driving the car every day to and from work—even went on vacation in it. My wife would use either the '64 GP or the GTO to take the kids to school or to go shopping. Our "family cars" were doing double duty on the dragstrip.

The GTO ran in F/S auto class, so I had to get it as close to the national record as I could. I kept working on the carb, and must have tried ten sets of jets and metering rods to get the best time out of it. I got it down to 12.6 @ 118 mph and never had the heads off the car. The class record was 11.9, but if you lived in a different part of the country than the record holder, you could still win. The reason was simple: not many guys ran on the record. It seemed like we were all a few tenths off. There were a couple guys that ran on it, but they were spread all over the country. It was like that in all the classes, so if they were not there, then the guy that was closest would win.

Racing was an unsafe sport at times. A friend that I went to school with blew a tire, rolled five times, and was killed. This made me pause and think about the whole drag racing thing, but I just could not stop. Every Saturday we went racing. My wife and daughter started a fan club, so to speak. There were about twenty of us and we all wore the same hats and jackets. Little did I know at the time this was the start of something a lot bigger than I ever dreamed it would be.

THE BEST LAID PLANS OF MICE AND MEN

What would your wife do if you bought a new car and never drove it on the street? The GTO had been a pretty good race car. In the course of a couple of years, I won a number of trophies and a Florida State championship. But like always, the need for speed was taking me over. The GTO was at the end of its run because I still had to drive it daily. Now I needed something new. I bought a brand spanking new 1969 Firebird and took it right into the shop and made a drag car out of it. I called this "testing a marriage."

When drag racing was running classes, it was best to sit down and figure out what car fit in what class and would have the best chance to win. You had to figure the weight of the car compared with horsepower and what class it would fall in. NHRA worked out the classes by the base weight of the car and the engine horsepower rating. The thing you had to be careful of was that NHRA would re-rate an engine if they thought the factory had rated it wrong. I guess that is why small-block Chevys had to run in the same class as big-block Fords. This was when I started to understand just how far Ford would go to win a race. I owned a lot of Fords and never thought about it one way or the other. But when you started to read the rulebook, it was a real eye opener. I will not linger on this too long and do not want to make anyone mad, but facts are facts. I will just say this: a

four-door Taurus with two doors looks like a Dodge in the front and a Monte Carlo in the rear. I think that says it all. Anyway, it took some planning to find a class you could win in.

After a lot of research, the Firebird had a base weight of 3,150 pounds and the Ram Air engine was rated at 345 hp. That turned out to be a real good combo to race in the S/SFA class. So I ordered a '69 Firebird, with a benchseat and column shift—the true base car. I ordered the Ram Air 500 engine with a 400 trans and a 4.33 Posi rear axle—all factory order stuff. Boy, it would be nice to still be able to do that! I was working for GM and got the car at cost, for $3,457. The car was delivered and I pulled it into the garage and started taking it apart. Trust me—this really drew a whole bunch of people to watch. I could hear a lot of talk about how crazy I was to take a new car apart.

I took the engine apart first and found some interesting things inside. The factory called for zero deck clearance on the block, but I had to take 42-thousandths off to bring it to zero. To bring the heads to the factory cc's, I had to mill them off 62-thousandths. That means that between the block and the heads, it took 104-thousandths to bring them to factory specs! I had the crankshaft polished and 1-thousandth taken off each side of all the rods. I took the camshaft to Crane Cams and had it checked just to find out that no two cylinders were the same. I had Harvey Crane cut me a camshaft that would have all the cylinders the same. As you can see by now, the factory specs on paper were a lot different than what came under the hood.

I got a set of Hooker headers. I put a 3,500-rpm stall converter and a shift kit in the 400 trans. All I did to the rear axle was to put special oil in it. I added Lakewood bars on the rear and installed 90-10 shocks on the front and 50-50 on the rear. I took everything off the car that did nothing, then put the car back together. I got a set of chrome wheels and a set of Goodyear slicks. I had to sell the Pontiac GP because I needed to buy a trailer and Chevy pickup truck.

Finally, I loaded up the Firebird and was ready to go try this baby out. Well, it's hard to believe, but for the next three weekends it rained! Here I was with my new race car on the trailer hooked to my new truck and I could not go racing. Finally, on the

fourth Saturday the weather was nice and we got to go racing.

Everyone's heard the saying, "the best laid plans of mice and men. . . ." Well, I was about to find out exactly what that saying meant.

I backed the race car off the trailer to warm up the oils. It had been running about five minutes when suddenly the carb flooded. I took the top off the carb and it had a piece of trash in the needle and seat. I fixed the carb and finished warming up the car. I took it to the line and waited for my turn, which seemed like forever. The burnouts felt like it had 200 more horsepower than the GTO; I could feel the car hitting the stops, it lifted so hard. I found out later that it was lifting the right front tire off the ground. I know you see that all the time now, but back then that was big time. I got the tires warmed up and went and staged the car. I hit the line lock and got the revs up to 3,500 against the converter. The lights came down; I released the line lock and slammed the gas pedal to the floor and *KA-BOOM!* all hell broke loose. The car turned sideways and made more noise than you could believe. It finally came to rest and I was in shock. I got out and could not believe what I saw. The new engine was as good as it sounded. It had so much torque that it ripped the tires off the rims. It killed the tubes, bent the rims, and also bent the rear fenders on my new race car. This was a whole new ballgame, when you had to put screws through the rims and into the tires to keep from turning the tires on the rims. This baby had some power! I never had to do this with the Flatheads of the Y-block Fords. Not knowing something just cost me a set of tires, tubes, and a lot of bodywork—and my new car didn't even have 5 miles on it.

Now, I was left sitting in the middle of the track with two bad tires, two torn-up rims, two bad tubes, and some bent fenders. This is the kind of stuff that happens to guys that get more power than they know what to do with. Of course, after it happened there were plenty of guys that said, "You should have asked. . . ." The thing was, these same guys walked around the car before I made the first run. If they knew so much and were willing to tell me, why is it they didn't say anything? There was a lesson to be learned by all of this.

I fixed the fenders and got new tires and rims. Now remember, after I got the car built, it rained for

a few weeks and then I messed up the car, so it had been well over a month and I had not even made the first run in the car.

I had the car in the garage that Saturday morning, getting it ready to race. I started up the car and was checking something, when Ruby came out of the house, waving her arms. I knew she was screaming because I could see her lips moving, even though I couldn't hear her. I turned the car off and she was in the doorway saying, "Come here, boy." I knew by the look on her face this was not good. I went into the house through the door to the kitchen. Oh, boy! All the cabinet doors were open and the dishes were on the floor. All the stuff that was hanging on the walls was also on the floor. One more lesson learned: you don't run a high-horsepower car with open headers in a closed garage. I was real lucky to be able to go to the track, because Ruby could have killed me. We also had to eat off paper plates for days.

The national record in my class was 11.38, and the first run I made on the new Firebird was 11.69 @ 128 mph. It was a shocker to be that close to the record the first time out. I won my class, got third in eliminations on the first night out, and was in the middle of eliminations for the next year. The car really had what it takes.

We pulled the car to Palm Beach one Saturday for the Southeast Nationals. Eliminations paid $2,500—a lot of money in 1970. There had to be 200 cars running for the Super Stock title. It took a long time to fight through all the rounds of cars. In your own class, it was all head-up racing, and then when it got to eliminations, it was kind of like ET brackets except they went by class record times instead of dial-in times. I had made my way through my class and to my surprise, all of a sudden I was in the finals. I was already spending the money. You see, the car that I was to run was a '64 Ford with a 427 engine. He had broken something in the round before and it sounded like he was on six cylinders, backfiring through the headers. But the rules said he had to make the run to get second-place money.

Well, as always, I could not leave well enough alone. It came to my mind that this would be a good time to try to set the national record because it paid an extra $1,000. So here was the deal: to win paid $2,500 and if I could set the record that would be $3,500 in one run. I hadn't made that much hauling moonshine just a few years back. I was really jacked up; this would be the biggest payday I had ever gotten racing. I went back in the pits and checked everything. I gave it just a little more timing and set the secondaries to open sooner. I knew I could beat the broken Ford, and even if it slowed me up a little, it would not hurt. But I was hoping that the changes would give me just a little more and I could set the record. I think I have hinted at this before: the best laid plans of mice and men quickly go astray.

They called us to the line and the time had come to go get my money. I heard that Ford coming—*POW, POW, POP, POP!* I always did one burnout, but the heck with tire wear: I was going for a record. I did three burnouts and staged. The guy in the Ford did not even do a burnout for fear he wouldn't be able to make the run. He needed to be able to make the run and get the money so he could fix his car. I found out later that he had missed a shift and bent some valves—not a lot of rev limiters in those days.

We staged, the lights came down, and my Firebird launched so hard I saw red. Oh, no! The red I saw was a red light! My greed just cost me first-place money to a guy that had to coast across the line. I would never live this down, and to this day, Ruby and my brother-in-law still remind me of that night.

I went around and picked up the time slip. There was no record time, not that it would have mattered. I drove around to the pits and parked the car, and boy, was it quiet. I went over to the pay window and Art handed me a check. I looked at it and it was for $2,500. Wow, second place paid the same as first! Then Art took the check back and said, "Oh no, you are the guy that red lighted." Of course, everyone had fun with that and the guy in the Ford offered to buy me a beer. Well, second place paid $1,480, so I only lost $1,020 plus a championship.

Boy, was the ride home quiet.

It was a real good lesson on greed, because most of the time this is how it turns out. By the way, the next year I did not red light and won the Southeast Nationals.

PAID TO RACE

The next thing I knew, I was racing around the country—and getting paid for it. I was working for Pontiac and drawing a weekly paycheck to go racing. It seemed too good to be true. Back in those days,

the factories were big on racing their cars. Some of the large dealerships like Royal in Michigan even ran cars all over the country. I had a Chevy with a camper on it and the plan was to spend every other night in the camper and the rest of the time in motels. So Ruby and I packed up to head north on a three-month adventure.

Our first stop was Orlando, Florida. The city didn't have a speedway at this time, just a small track, but it was on the way. I made three runs and was getting into the money rounds. I had run the right lane all night and then drew the left lane. As I soon discovered, at the end of the left lane there was a large dip and when I hit it, the car bottomed out and broke the left Hooker header.

Back then, Hooker was the god of headers but Orlando was small time; Mickey Mouse had not yet come to Florida and ruined the state. I couldn't find another Hooker header until I got to Jacksonville. I will tell you right now that until you try to change a header on a Firebird on a trailer without a lift you have not truly lived and suffered. Finally I got smart and went to a Pontiac dealer to use a lift after hours. Now I had plenty of help: a couple mechanics, the shop foreman, and even the owner stopped by to lend a hand. There were a lot of guys in dealerships in those days that raced, and the shop foreman even had Ruby and me over to his house for dinner. He was a local racer, and we had a hard time leaving because he wanted to talk racing all night long.

The next morning, we started out through Georgia. There were a couple tracks worth racing that paid what we called "pull money." As the weeks went by, we got a new respect for the guys that did this all the time. Instead of every other night in the camper, we were often so far away from civilization that we were forced to camp every night there. Still, we were making money at about two out of every three tracks we raced.

There was a track in Dayton, Ohio, and here we ran into one of those strange deals. The race was a major event and I had made about eight runs. It got down to me and a Road Runner in the finals for the big money. I did my normal thing—a burnout, staged, held the line lock, the lights came down, and away we went. It was a pretty normal race and I won by just a bit. At the end, the guy in the Road Runner stopped to talk to me. He was still there and helping me line up the Firebird to put on the trailer when *BAM!* a right axle broke. We got the car on the trailer, and then what happened is still hard to believe. The guy's name was Art Watson, and he took us to his house and we stayed in a room over his garage for two nights. I used his garage and equipment to fix the broken axle—and he wouldn't take any money at all. I had just won $980 by beating him at the track, and here he was helping me out. Art was a real racer and a good person; I miss things like that.

We were racing at Lyons Dragway when Big Daddy Don blew the clutch and lost his toes. We all know the end of this story: we now have rear-engine dragsters. Back in those early days of drag racing, you saw some strange things—two-engine dragsters, four-engine ones, and if you were around to see the first funny cars you'd know how they got their name.

We had been in about eight states so far and had done well. I don't think I could have made a living drag racing but being paid my salary made it easy. We had been out for almost two months and after all the payouts, we still were money ahead just from the winnings. We were at Englishtown and had a close call—the racer in the other lane lost control, crossed the center line, and just tipped my rear bumper. It did no damage but it upset me enough that I red lighted the next round, which was the final. I really don't know if that was the reason for my red light this time, but the story worked and everyone believed me.

Even though this drag racing was a lot of fun and I met a lot of nice people, we did get tired of the road. Still, I wouldn't have traded it for anything. In all, we raced thirty-two tracks up and down the East Coast—strips like Lyons and Englishtown and a lot of tracks that are long gone. We were out almost three months, and besides oil changes, tune ups, the broken header and axle, we had no other trouble. Your luck simply couldn't get much better than that. By the end of the road trip, we had banked around $4,500. Besides being paid my salary, I got half the winnings after everything was paid for.

Looking back at all my racing, I don't think it was ever as much fun as that summer. When they started ET bracket racing, it just wasn't like the early days. And then when they took the racer out of the mix and began using computers, the best mechanic and racer didn't always win anymore. I went on to take a couple more state championships and one more southern one, but after about 1975, it was never the same again. The big-dollar boys kind of pushed out the little guy.

Looking back, I wouldn't change any of it. I had a lot of fun, met a lot of nice and also famous people, and saw a lot of places. If any of you ever get the chance to go racing, don't even think about it. Just do it.

CHAPTER 4

GOW JOBS

I got a date with my baby about a half past eight;
I don't have to worry, she won't be late.
We're going downtown where the cats all meet,
We're going downtown to drag Main Street!
–Curtis Gordon, "Draggin'," 1956

CRUISE NIGHT: A street rod parks at Nick's Drive-In in this painting by Kent Bash. (Artwork © Kent Bash)

Annette
MUSCLE BEACH PARTY

SONGS FROM THE
AMERICAN INTERNATIONAL FILM
PLUS
MERLIN JONES
THE
SCRAMBLED EGGHEAD

ANNETTE'S BOSS VERSIONS OF

DRAGGIN' U.S.A.
SHUTDOWN AGAIN

CUSTOM CITY
REBEL RIDER

Surf **Rods**

By Pat Ganahl

Growing up in California, Pat Ganahl was smitten by surfing from early on. He built his own boards and learned to ride the breaks alongside many surfing legends.

In this essay, Pat details the relationship between the surfing scene and hot rodding, from styles and fads to the unique automotive requirements of surfers. Both surfing and rodding grew up primarily in Southern California, sharing influences and swapping styles along the way. In large part from the music of the likes of Dick Dale and the Beach Boys, riding the long boards and drag racing became inseparably mixed as an icon of Americana.

Pat still owns the '48 Chevy he describes here as his first surf rod. And it still wears the United States Surfing Association decal that he affixed to the rear side window in 1963.

SURF ROD: Surfing and hot rods went together like rock and roll. Whether it was Dick Dale and his Fender Stratocaster blasting out "Miserlou" at the Rendevous Ballroom or the Beach Boys' sugary sweet pop tunes, they all sang the praises of surf rods. Reformed Mouseketeer Annette Funicello symbolized surfing beach parties to many across the country from her series of exploitation movies and tie-in soundtrack LPs, such as *Muscle Beach Party* from 1964. She may not truly have known which side of a longboard to stand on, but she was without doubt America's surfing sweetheart.

It was an era of fads and crazes. Maybe it started with the Hula Hoop and progressed to the Frisbee (originally the Pluto Platter, remember?). But it seemed like every couple of months it was something new, and every teen had to be in on it if they wanted to be up-to-the-minute "with it."

Clothes were a big part of it. Hot rodders liked T-shirts and jeans, but you couldn't wear Levis to school. So we had Peggers; then those pants with the straps and buckle in the back; then the button-down Ivy League look. Remember those really skinny belts—white or maybe chrome—and if you were tough you wore the buckle to the side? Then came those super skinny ties, and shirts with a snap at the collar to make the tie stand out. Hairdos: jelly rolls and ducktails (D.A.'s); then flattops with fenders; then the Ivy League cut.

How about the model-car craze? We started making hot rod and custom models from those little Highway Pioneers kits, using parts from the Revell jalopy or hot rod roadster. Then AMT caught on and introduced the "3-in-1" customizing kits in '58. Suddenly we had monthly model-car contests at the hobby shop, model-car displays at car shows, the Revell/Pactra national model-car contest, and several model-car magazines. By the second half of the 1960s, most of this was over.

Then we had the ten-speed bicycle craze. Suddenly—I think it was in 1961—every kid had to have one, either a Schwinn or something from Italy. I couldn't afford the $110 they cost, so I made my own

out of spare parts. First it was Honduras Maroon, then it was Fawn Beige with a black tuck-and-roll seat. I even got a weekend job assembling and repairing ten-speeds at the TV shop next to the drugstore where I worked after school. TVs and ten-speeds—why not?

Of course, hot rodding itself was fad-driven during this era of the late 1950s and early 1960s. Unlike today, when you can build a rod or custom in the style of any era you want, back then everybody had to follow the latest trend or fad. First, we had wide whitewalls, then medium whitewalls, then narrow whitewalls (remember U.S. Royal Masters?). In my area, cars (we just called them cars, not rods or customs) went from flipper wheelcovers (Olds Fiesta three-bar or Dodge Lancer four-bar), to baby moons (beanies, baldies) and beauty rims, to chrome reversed rims, to mag wheels (or much-cheaper Raders). Then Hurst convinced everybody they needed a floorshift, and Sun and Dixco got everybody to mount a tach on the dash. Upholstery went from white tuck-and-roll, to black tuck-and-roll, to sculptured black tuck-and-roll with narrow one-inch pleats, to (yuck!) black diamond-tuck (also called diamond-tuft or button-tuck). Then everybody had to have a tarp over the backseat (with a tuck-and-roll diamond in the middle or a "weirdo" monster painted on it) and a tuck-and-roll package tray. Pipes were a more regional thing, but the trend kept changing. Where I was, they went from lakes pipes to cheaters or scavengers under the rear axle. In other parts of town, Bellflower tips behind the rear wheels were the pipes of choice. I could go on and on.

Perhaps the trendiest things of all during this era were the dance steps. Everybody remembers the twist and the stroll. But how about the swim, the fly, the pony, the locomotion, and the mashed potato—to name just a few? Each had its specific steps and arm movements, and you had to watch Dick Clark or Lloyd Thaxton after school to see how each was done so you wouldn't be uncool at the next sock hop. Actually, the girls were usually the only ones who could do the fast dances, so they danced with each other while we pitched pennies in the corner, waiting for the next slow dance. And then came the surfer's stomp. That changed everything. I'd peg it right around 1962, maybe a little earlier. The actual song, "Surfer's Stomp" by the Markettes, was released in November 1961, but was never a big hit.

Surfing had been around in California since the 1920s and in Hawaii well before that. But during 1961 and 1962, it suddenly broke out as a giant craze, beginning, of course, in Southern California. And the actual riding of surfboards was only a small part of it. There were plenty of "surfers" who never surfed. The music was a major part of it—perhaps the spark that lit the surfing fuse. And I'm not talking the Beach Boys. When the Beach Boys made a rare appearance at the Rendezvous Ballroom in Balboa, my friends and I refused to go. They dressed in silly matching outfits—red striped Ivy League shirts—sang like girls, and didn't even surf. No, we went to Dick Dale dances. He truly was King of the Surf Guitar—still is. With the reverb and the volume both cranked to the limit and that gold Metalflake Strat throbbing and screaming, you could literally feel the pulsing of the music as you walked in the door. And the surfer's stomp really was a two-beat stomp, so pretty soon the whole floor was bouncing in rhythm to the music—especially at the wooden-floored Rendezvous. We also saw Dick surfing with us at the beach. And his surf music wasn't about surfer girls, sidewalk surfing, or woodies in the snow. He mainly did amped-up early R&B jewels: "Night Owl," "Fanny Mae," "Lovey Dovey," "Peppermint Man," "Summertime Blues," "Boney Moronie." Of course, Dick played at other places like Harmony Park in Anaheim and local armories (even in my little hometown a few times), and we followed the circuit. And there were other reverb-guitar-driven surf bands that played dances, such as the Chantays, the Challengers, Dave Myers and the Surftones, the Surfaris, the Torquays, and the Tornadoes.

Then there was the look—and this was a major departure from the styles of hair and clothing that preceded it. The hair: long, loose, straight (no grease!), and bleached blond from all that sun (if not from something else). The uniform: white Levis (really an off-white, which for some reason were allowed at school), a "bleeding" madras plaid shirt, a plaid Pendleton outer-shirt or jacket, Jack Purcell tennis shoes, and accessories like a St. Christopher medal on a chain around your neck or on the dashboard of your car. Another insignia that got connected to surfing, for who knows what reason, was the iron cross, such as the one used by Schneider Cams as a logo today.

But don't for a minute think that everybody joined in this surf craze. In the eighth grade, I was using pomade and had a hairdo to rival Kookie Byrnes. In the ninth grade, I got bit by the surfing bug, changed my hairstyle completely, and built my first board. When I entered high school the next year, with my hair longer and blonder, I literally got my butt kicked the first day. I turned around to see a circle of seniors from the varsity football team, most with flattops or oily jelly-roll hair. Fortunately, they sicked the shortest guy on me, who announced, "I say surfers eat shit." I immediately retorted, "Well, I say greasers eat shit." We stood and glared at each other a while, and then the big guys figured I hadn't chickened out, so they let me go. In surf parlance (of which there was plenty), "greaser" was not a racial epithet, but referred to guys who put grease in their hair—non-surfers. As is too often the case with teenagers, there was plenty of that us-versus-them attitude.

One of the things that made for common ground, however, was cars. Nearly all the guys who joined the surf cult in '62 or so were hot rodders to one degree or another, simply because most male teens of the latter 1950s and early 1960s were into cars. My immediate group of friends (most of whom were about five years older than I was and therefore had cars way before I did) were big-time rodders well before the surf thing went huge. Ronnie had a Cad-powered, black lacquer '51 Ford. Russell had a dual-quad 301 Chevy-powered Forty coupe with a Hydro. Wally had a Model A coupe

Right, **READY FOR THE BREAKS:** Author Pat Ganahl, young and barefoot, packs his boards on a homemade rack atop his '48 rod and gets ready to head for the beach. He sanded the car to paint it Naples Orange, but—perhaps fortunately, he says now—he never got that far during high school. The top board was made of balsa; his dad broke off the fin while trying to learn to surf. (Pat Ganahl collection)

and then a 265-powered '53 Chevy convertible with blue and white T. J. tuck-and-roll. John had a cinnamon-red '50 Ford business coupe that we put a couple of tri-carb Flatheads in and for which I built hairpin-style traction bars in metal shop.

Since we were rodders, when we got into surfing we had a do-it-yourself mentality and we all built our own surfboards in our parents' garages. We even had our own label. And, being rodders, we all had to customize our boards. Mine had a redwood iron cross inlaid in the skeg (fin). Ronnie (who later became a professional board builder) made his own unique-shaped skeg from laminated woods. Russell (who became an artist) sort of sculpted his foam blank into an artistic shape that didn't ride for beans.

In the early 1960s, typical surfboard length was about 9 feet, 6 inches (which we called a "nine six"). Plus, they weighed more than 30 pounds. Getting these things to the beach, especially if the gang was going together, was a problem. A Model A or Forty coupe wasn't going to cut it. So my buddies sold their regular rods and bought things like "panels" (really sedan deliveries), two-door wagons, or other large vehicles you could either put surfboards inside, or put plenty of people in, with the boards on top on a rack. But being hot rodders to begin with, we couldn't leave these vehicles stock.

Of course, the quintessential surf rod is a '40s Ford or Mercury woodie wagon. There were quite a few around the beaches, to be sure, but we certainly couldn't afford one. Most of them belonged to the older guys. In the 1962-1965 period when I was in high school, there were two five-window Deuce coupes in the parking lot, a couple of '55 Chevys (jacked up in the front, no bumper, American mags), one new red 409 Chevy that someone's dad bought him, and one 4-4-2 Olds that the guy bought himself, but the vast majority were 1949-1957 "somethings"—Chevys, Fords, Oldses, Pontiacs, whatever. So, we naturally leaned toward the same sort of vehicles for surf rods.

Ronnie got a '54 Ford delivery, faded red, that he put a 390 Ford engine and four-speed in. He was working as a mechanic at the time, so it was pretty hot, and he did plenty of street racing when he wasn't surfing. It ran Casler cheater slicks on the street and had an iron cross painted on the lower right of the back door. Russ got a '55 Ford delivery with a six and three-speed in it, painted it metallic olive green,

upholstered it in black tuck-and-roll, and added chromed reversed wheels with blackwalls. Later John bought this, and he and I installed a 312 Mercury Y-block in it. Ronnie's younger brother Gregory got a very nice '57 Chevy two-door wagon that he also painted olive green (remember that era?), installed a 283 and Muncie four-speed in it, and fit it with unpolished American five-spoke mags. He waxed it every week. And Wally got a faded red '40 Ford sedan delivery with a blown engine and "Puerta de Emergencia" painted on the back door (like all the citrus pickers' buses in town) that I installed two Flatheads in—in my parents' driveway—but that he eventually sold because we could never figure out how to put a fan on it.

Other surfmobiles among our broader group of friends included a really nice, bright yellow '56 Ford two-door wagon with three carbs, T-bird valve covers, and ram's-horn manifolds on the hot 312 Y-block; another olive green '42 Chevy pickup with a handmade, shingled, wooden camper on the back; a black '55 Chevy two-door wagon, jacked up, no front bumper, with at least two American mags on it; a blue metallic '55 Ford F-100 pickup with chromed reversed rims and black tuck-and-roll; and my multicolored, partially primered '48 Chevy sedan with two carbs, Fenton headers, a homemade floorshift, and a tach on the dash. Oh yeah, and it had knotty pine paneling instead of door panels inside, because that's as close as I could get to owning a real woodie. It didn't get painted until after I graduated, but it carried plenty of surfboards to the beach, with lots of people inside, during my high school years. When it was guys and girlfriends, I put the boards (usually three or four) on top on homemade racks—only lost those boards once! Later, in college, when I usually went by myself, I folded the rear seat down and slid the board in through the trunk—only broke the right front windshield twice!

Other surf rods in our area included a black primered '48 Cadillac limousine that had greyhounds painted on the sides (like the buses); a slope-back pea-green '50 Plymouth sedan with chromed wheels; and a '57 Plymouth hardtop with a stock Flathead six. Most anything would do. Hearses were popular—if you could find one. And of course, they all had mattresses in the back. Mothers immediately saw these as rolling sex machines (and they weren't

Facing page, **CLASSIC HOT ROD ACCESSORIES**

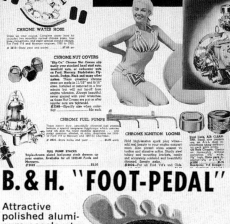

Hot Rods and Rock and Roll:
Odes to Acceleration and Hymns to Speed

Mississippi Delta bluesman Muddy Waters summed it up best when he said, "The blues had a baby and they called it rock and roll." But without an automobile, it's unlikely that baby would have gotten to the hospital on time.

Songs had been sung to cars before rock and roll. In 1905, a singer named Billy Murray recorded the first known song dedicated to his car, "In My Merry Oldsmobile," which hit the charts and hightailed it straight to number one. Bluesman Robert Johnson sang his "Terraplane Blues" way back in 1936 with thinly veiled sexual allusions between his Hudson Terraplane and his sweetheart. Other pioneering car songs included Jimmy Liggins' "Cadillac Boogie" and Connie Jordan and the Jordanaires' "Hot Rod Boogie" instrumental, both from 1947.

It was a 1951 hymn to an Oldsmobile called "Rocket 88" by Jackie Brenston and his Delta Cats that jumpstarted rock and roll. Brenston was the tenor saxman in Ike Turner's Kings of Rhythm band that was then tearing up the South. Recording at Sam Phillips' soon-to-be-famous Sun Studios in Memphis, Turner turned the mic over to Brenston to cut the supercharged tune with the perfect hot rod chorus:

Step in my Rocket and don't be late
Baby, we're pulling out about half past eight
Goin' round the corner and get a fifth
Everybody in my car's gonna take a little nip

Some historians call "Rocket 88" the first rock and roll song, but that's like trying to pinpoint the first hot rod. Regardless, it was hot and it rocked—and it set the tone for songs to come.

The fifties witnessed an explosion of car culture and rock and roll at the same time. In 1950, singer Arkie Shibley cut "Hot Rod Race," which sparked a slew of covers and imitators that hit the charts in the coming years.

Charlie Ryan followed with "Hot Rod Lincoln" in 1955, featuring Neal Livingston wringing from his steel guitar the sounds of sirens, acceleration, and whiplash. Ryan knew of what he sung. He was a true hot rodder who wrote the song in homage to his own machine, a '41 Lincoln Zephyr four-door sedan. Ryan pulled the body, sawed two feet off the frame to tighten the wheelbase, and replaced it with a '30 Model A Ford coupe body. He then installed a '48 Lincoln V-12 engine backed by a three-speed-plus-overdrive '48 transmission. It was hot, and he sang its praises:

I looked in the mirror and a red light was blinkin'
The cops was after my Hot Rod Lincoln.
Well, they arrested me and put me in jail.
Called my pop to make my bail.
He said, "Son, you're gonna drive me to drinkin'
If you don't quit drivin' that Hot Rod Lincoln!"

"Hot Rod Lincoln" inspired hot rodders and rock and rollers everywhere—it seemed like the cars and the music were custom-built for each other. Chuck Berry stepped up with his "motorvatin'" hit "Maybellene" in 1955. Nervous Norvus cut "Transfusion" in 1956, a bizarre ukulele-accompanied saga of automobile crack-ups and the resultant blood-loss:

Transfusion, transfusion!
Oh, nurse I'm gonna make a new resolution:
I'm never, never, never gonna speed again.
Put a gallon in me, Alan!

The Playmates played "Beep Beep," Ronnie Dee launched "Action Packed," and Robert Mitchum sang "The Ballad of Thunder Road" in 1958. And so it went. From "The Little Old Lady from Pasadena" to "Three Window Coupe" to "409," Jan and Dean, the Rip Chords, the Beach Boys, and many more

GENE VINCENT: Gene Vincent sang many a hymn to hot rodding, from his classic "Race with the Devil" to the soundtrack for the hot rod exploitation flick, *Hot Rod Gang*. The first hot rodders may have listened to jazz, but by the mid-1950s, rock and roll was the musical drug of choice—and to many, Vincent and His Blue Caps were the best of the best.

hot-wired their hymns to hot rodding in the coming years. Rock and roll seemed as vital to hot rods as gasoline.

The Beach Boys might have burned rubber up the hit charts more times, but they never truly captured the sound of hot rodding the way one man and his own hot-rodded Fender Stratocaster electric guitar did. Dick Dale was a surfer, hot rodder, and guitar picker that could channel all the excitement of a drag race through his amp. Fronting his band, the Del-Tones, Dale's tunes such as "The Scavenger" and "Mr. Eliminator" were loud and fast and dangerous—just like a real hot rod.

To an older generation, the overdriven roar of hot rods and electric guitars meant trouble. Weaned on the sugar-sweet crooning of Bing Crosby and the like, it's little wonder that fast cars and fast music sounded a wake-up call against juvenile delinquency for parents and the establishment. Films like *Rebel without a Cause* and reels upon reels of driver's-ed horror flicks offered morality tales to teens, but most teens were instead listening to the music that glorified the cars and the speed and the noise.

Hot rod and rock and roll might both have existed without the other, but they sure wouldn't have been the same. —Michael Dregni

BOSS DRAG THE T-BONES
HEY LITTLE COBRA ✦ SHUT DOWN
LITTLE DEUCE COUPE ✦ DRAG CITY
REVVIN' BUGGY ▪ BIG DADDY STOCKER ▪ DRAGGIN' ▪ SIX-BANGER ▪ TORQUE ROD ▪ SCORCHIN' ▪ RAIL-VETTE ▪ BOSS DRAG

LIBERTY
LRP-3346

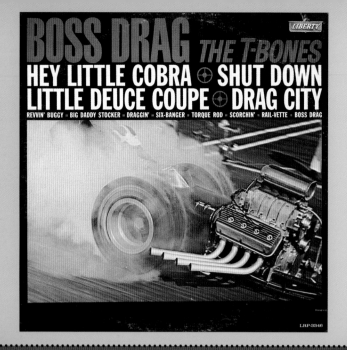

COLUMBIA
"devil woman" MARTY ROBBINS

DEVIL WOMAN ▪ AIN'T LIFE A CRYING SHAME ▪ TIME CAN'T MAKE ME FORGET
IN THE ASHES OF AN OLD LOVE AFFAIR ▪ THE HANDS YOU'RE HOLDING NOW ▪ WORRIED
LITTLE RICH GIRL ▪ PROGRESSIVE LOVE ▪ I'M BEGINNING TO FORGET
LOVE IS A HURTING THING ▪ KINDA HALFWAY FEEL ▪ THE WINE FLOWED FREELY

GUARANTEED
HIGH FIDELITY

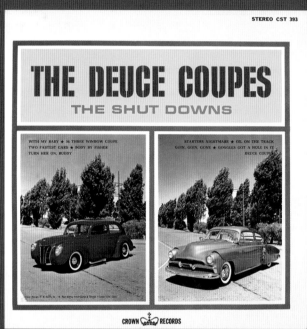

STEREO CST 393

THE DEUCE COUPES
THE SHUT DOWNS

WITH MY BABY ★ 36 THREE WINDOW COUPE
TWO FASTEST CARS ★ BODY BY FISHER
TURN HER ON, BUDDY

STARTERS NIGHTMARE ★ OIL ON THE TRACK
GOIN, GOIN, GONE ★ GOGGLES GOT A HOLE IN IT
DEUCE COUPE

CROWN RECORDS

JAN & DEAN take LINDA SURFIN'

LINDA ● MR. BASS MAN ● SURFIN' SAFARI ● RHYTHM OF THE RAIN ● WALK LIKE A MAN
● THE BEST FRIEND I EVER HAD ● MY FOOLISH HEART ● SURFIN' ● THE GYPSY CRIED ●
●● WALK RIGHT IN ●●● LET'S TURKEY TROT ●●● WHEN I LEARN HOW TO CRY ●●

LIBERTY

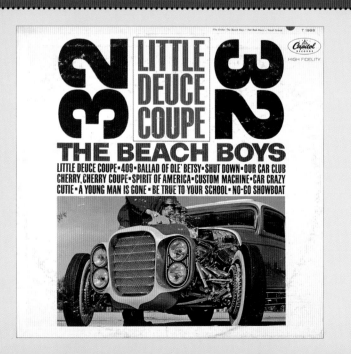

Capitol Records
HIGH FIDELITY

32 LITTLE DEUCE COUPE 32
THE BEACH BOYS

LITTLE DEUCE COUPE ▪ 409 ▪ BALLAD OF OLE' BETSY ▪ SHUT DOWN ▪ OUR CAR CLUB
CHERRY, CHERRY COUPE ▪ SPIRIT OF AMERICA ▪ CUSTOM MACHINE ▪ CAR CRAZY
CUTIE ▪ A YOUNG MAN IS GONE ▪ BE TRUE TO YOUR SCHOOL ▪ NO-GO SHOWBOAT

T 1998

DEUCES, "T's," ROADSTERS & DRUMS
HAL BLAINE
(THE DRUMMER MAN)
And The Young Cougars

Challenger II ▪ Green Monster ▪ Nashville Coupe
Big "T" ▪ Mr. Eliminator ▪ Pop the Chute ▪ Deuces, "T's," Roadsters & Drums ▪ Drum Brakes
Gear Change ▪ The Phantom Driver ▪ Gear Stripper ▪ The Traps

RCA VICTOR
DYNAGROOVE
RECORDING

LPM-2834

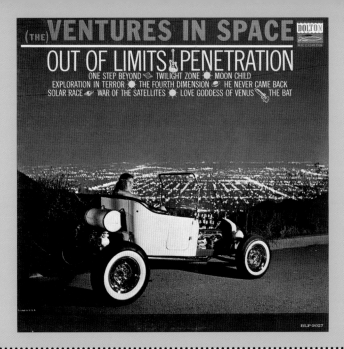

(THE) VENTURES IN SPACE
DOLTON RECORDS

OUT OF LIMITS | PENETRATION
ONE STEP BEYOND ● TWILIGHT ZONE ● MOON CHILD
EXPLORATION IN TERROR ● THE FOURTH DIMENSION ● HE NEVER CAME BACK
SOLAR RACE ● WAR OF THE SATELLITES ● LOVE GODDESS OF VENUS ● THE BAT

BLP-2027

WILD, EXCITING, NEW—MUSIC OF THE TRACKS—ACTUAL SOUNDS

THE TOKENS

SHORT JUMP
LACQUERED CHOPPER
PISTON KING BEAT
T-BONE STRAIGHT
HIGH BOY DREAM

KING'S OF THE HOT RODS

WHEELER DEALER
'34 CHOPPER
ACEY DUECE
WING DING
HOT VELTE

PLUS INSTRUMENTALS BY HAL JONES & THE WHEELERS

MONO 2308

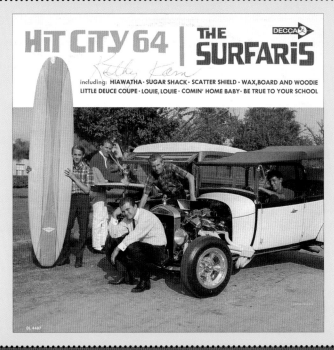

HIT CITY 64 | THE SURFARIS
DECCA

including: HIAWATHA ● SUGAR SHACK ● SCATTER SHIELD ● WAX, BOARD AND WOODIE
LITTLE DEUCE COUPE ● LOUIE, LOUIE ● COMIN' HOME BABY ● BE TRUE TO YOUR SCHOOL

DL 4487

DRAG BEAT

THE DE-FENDERS
Side One: DEUCES WILD ● TACO WAGON ● MOVIN' AND
GROOVIN' ● SKIN DIVER ● LOOSE NUTS ● LITTLE DEUCE
COUPE ● Side Two: DRAG BEAT ● WHEELIN' HOME ● FOUR
BANGER ● TEQUILA JOE ● RUM RUNNER ● ROAD RUNNER

DEL-FI RECORDS

A BOB KEENE PRODUCTION

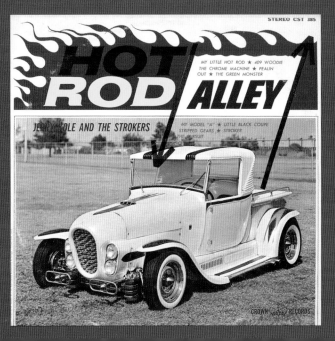

STEREO CST 385

HOT ROD ALLEY

MY LITTLE HOT ROD ★ 409 WOODIE
THE CHROME MACHINE ★ PEALIN
OUT ★ THE GREEN MONSTER

JERRY COLE AND THE STROKERS

MY MODEL "A" ★ LITTLE BLACK COUPE
STRIPPED GEARS ★ STROKER
THE PURSUIT

CROWN RECORDS

STEREO CS 9016

THREE WINDOW COUPE
COLUMBIA

THREE WINDOW COUPE / THIS LITTLE WOODIE / GAS MONEY / BONNEVILLE BONNIE / HOT ROD U.S.A. / SURF CITY
SURFIN' CRAZE / BEACH GIRL / MY BIG GUN BOARD / OLD CAR MADE IN '52 / SUMMER U.S.A. / BIG WEDNESDAY

THE RIP CHORDS

Above, **WILD HOT ROD SOUNDS:** Capitol Records was just one of many labels eager to cash in on the craze for hot rod music, as shown in this 1964 ad.

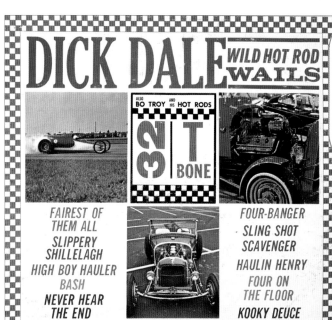

DICK DALE: Dick Dale (above) reveled in loudness, whether it was the roar of a surfing wave, the sound of his turbocharged Fender Stratocaster, or the exhaust note of a hot rod. Dale was one of the unsung pioneering heroes of rock and roll, primarily because his early stages were confined to California beach towns where he could be near the best breaks at all times. Dale's LP *Wild Hot Rod Wails* was advertised as leading the charge into a new trend of "hot rod music."

completely incorrect), but the initial reason for them was to protect the surfboards and to allow overnight sleeping at the beach.

My dad had a '54 Ford two-door wagon at that time, and he let me plaster the back windows with surfboard decals. That was enough to make it a "sorta" surf rod, and I'd borrow it to take to the beach (especially when my own car was broken). It even had a mattress in the back—for my dad's ski trips.

My hometown at that time was about fifty miles from the beach, so surf trips were relatively major undertakings. The cars had to be somewhat reliable (I carried lots of spare parts in the trunk), and that's why we piled as many people as possible in one car. But a typical surf trip might entail 250 miles in a day. And there were no freeways then. For one thing, you had to find good surf. We'd go from break to break, always looking for something better. Or we'd decide that we had to go to one of the well-known good surf spots, like Rincon up near Santa Barbara, or Steamer Lane all the way up in Santa Cruz, or down to Swami's near San Diego, or even into Mexico. This is why you had a mattress in the back.

You'd see all kinds of cars with surfboards on top or hanging out the back trolling up and down the Pacific Coast Highway, especially on weekends. If the surf was bad, there would be twice as many cars on the road, looking for better spots. If the surf was good, you'd see surf rods lined up by the side of the highway, along the cliffs, or in parking lots at the well-known breaks.

One of our favorite-surfing spots—and Dick Dale's too (he wrote a song about it)—was called Mile Zero. The name came because there used to be a speedometer check there on PCH, and we parked on the cliff, next to the "Mile 0" sign. It's now part of San Onofre State Park, but back then it was part of the Camp Pendleton Marine base, which was technically off limits to surfers. If the Marines caught you on the beach, they'd confiscate your surfboard; if you were in the water, they couldn't get you. We'd park on the dirt, next to the highway, and then have to walk down a steep path from the cliffs to the beach. One time we came up the cliff when we were done surfing to find three or four other surfers looking over a

very nice, yellow '55 Ford tudor wagon with some sort of custom wheels. One of the guys was identifying this as the car that belonged to someone who had wronged him in some way recently, and they started picking up big rocks and smashing all the windows out of it. They asked if we wanted to join in, and we declined, backing off quickly. This was an unfortunate part of the surf-rod era that was not uncommon. I heard one story about some hot rod "greasers" who went around beach towns in an F-100 pickup with a cutting torch in the back, cutting holes in woodies and other surf rods, but I don't think it was true.

Of course the surfers who actually lived in the beach towns didn't have to make pilgrimages to the beach and could have wilder cars. Back in the early 1950s, when I lived in a beach town, one of the first hot rods I ever saw was a '29 Model A roadster pickup. I think it was black primered, and I know it was full of high school kids, guys and girls. But it had wood posts in the bed rails, with a flat roof over the bed and cab, covered in big palm fronds like a thatched roof—sort of a rolling beach hut. It might not have been a surf rod, but it was definitely a beach rod.

And then, all of a sudden, the craze was over. We kept surfing, sure. But the Beatles invaded the airwaves, and Bob Dylan and Joan Baez started singing protest songs. The real surf bands disappeared—as did dancing, for the most part—and the pop bands like the Beach Boys, Jan and Dean, the Rip Chords, even Dick Dale, ironically turned to hot rods or drag racing as the subject for new albums. Surfers' hair got longer and longer as the boards got shorter and shorter. And hot rods pretty much disappeared altogether, while surf rods turned into flower-painted VW microbuses, and then into vans.

People talk about 1960s as if it were one decade, but it wasn't. It was two completely distinct semidecades. For the zillions of us baby boomers who were born in the 1940s, grew up in the 1950s, went to high school in the first half of the 1960s, possibly went to college in the second half of the 1960s, and became (more or less) adult by the end of that decade, it was an amazing, and ultimately eye-opening, time to mature. Hot rods, surfboards, rock and roll—I'm sure glad to have been part of it all.

Thunder and Lightning:
From Ridge Runners to HOT RODS

By Brad Bowling

Brad Bowling is an automotive journalist and photographer who has authored several histories and recently finished writing the twenty-year story of the Saleen Mustang. He has been the editor of *Old Cars Weekly* and *Mustang Times*, a member of the board of directors of the Mustang Club of America, the public relations coordinator for Saleen Autosport, and associate editor of *Mustang Illustrated*.

Some historians become jaded by the sheer number of amazing cars they drive, write about, and photograph. Not so Brad. He remains an enthusiast at heart.

In this essay, Brad examines the roots of southern hot rod culture and the legendary influence of the moonshining "ridge runners."

RIDGE RUNNER: Nostalgia for the glory days of moonshining inspired the building of this '49 Ford coupe ridge runner. Original moonshine-hauling cars were purposebuilt hot rods made by cutting away any unnecessary weight and bulk, hopping up engines, tightening suspension for driving the ridges and mountain roads, and making room in the interiors and trunks for 120 to 150 gallons of white lightning. (Photograph © Brad Bowling)

White lightning, alley bourbon, rotgut, hillbilly pop, city gin, mountain dew—these are just a few of the names the corn liquor produced in illegal stills throughout the southeastern United States has gone by during the last 200-plus years. Like most contraband products, these euphemisms for what we generally know as "moonshine" originated as part of a coded language to be shared among members of the user community.

No matter what name you apply, the unstoppable underground alcohol industry that first became a political issue during the 1794 Whiskey Rebellion has given birth to a uniquely southern regional folklore, a successful movie and television genre all its own, and an automotive culture that runs the gamut from hot rods to stock cars.

TWO CENTURIES OF SUPPLY AND DEMAND

The whiskey excise tax of 1791 only cemented the fiercely independent us-versus-them attitude of the Scotch and Irish settlers who endured an introverted, poverty-level existence in the Blue Ridge Mountains, eastern Tennessee, and much of the Carolinas. Unwilling to turn over what little bounty the land provided to the federal government, many farmers developed techniques for secretly converting abundant corn—plus sugar, water, yeast, and malt—into a soupy mash and distilling it into a clear liquid. Cloak of night concealed the still's telltale smoke plume, which is how the term "moonshine"—a word first made popular in England and Europe to describe liquor smuggled in the dark—was applied to the product as well as the act of making it.

So strong was the resistance of the Carolina hill people to the first federal whiskey tax that even George Washington's army and U.S. Treasury Secretary Alexander Hamilton bypassed the area and concentrated on offenders in Pennsylvania.

Taxation of whiskey producers ended briefly in 1801, but the need to fund the War of 1812 caused a temporary revival of the sin tax, and fifty years later, after the financial drain of the Civil War, it was made a permanent part of the American economy. Seeking millions of dollars in unpaid tribute at the conclusion of the War between the States, the Treasury Department created a Revenue Bureau with police-like powers and jurisdictions whose "revenuer" agents were charged with putting moonshiners out of business and in jail.

Thus began in earnest the sometimes violent, but always colorful, conflict between the Treasury Department and the mountain-bred entrepreneurs who would have a strong impact on the popular culture of the South.

THUNDER IN THE MOUNTAINS

As the American industrial machine sped into the twentieth century, a church-driven movement to curb the drinking habits of the factory-laboring working class resulted in a state-by-state temperance campaign that in 1920 led to a decade-long national Prohibition against the manufacture, sale, or transportation of intoxicating liquors, with the passing of the 18th Amendment to the U.S. Constitution. Prohibition, its repeal, and fallout—liquor stores run by the government and voluntarily "dry" southern counties chief among them—only pushed the highly profitable home stills deeper into the mountains of the Carolinas, Tennessee, and Georgia.

Whether selling to a dry county or simply avoiding the federal tax, the success of the moonshiner's business relied on getting his product to a distributor or consumer without being detected by law enforcement officials. In the eighteenth century, an illegal whiskey maker's market was limited to short distances by a primitive transportation system consisting of horse-drawn carts on rugged roads and various watercraft. In the 1930s, with hidden stills working at maximum capacity to supply cheap alcohol to the major southern cities, bootleggers began using high-powered but nondescript passenger cars to transport their product. Although commercial-grade trucks could haul many times more volume, they were too easy a target for revenue agents to track and confiscate, and their use was limited. Ordinary Ford, Chevy, and Dodge automobiles were turned into purposebuilt ridge runners by removing unnecessary weight, modifying engines, and making room in the interiors and trunks for 120 to 150 gallons of white lightning.

Ford's flathead V-8 was the powerplant of choice with most transporters in the '30s. But once they became widely available, Cadillac's overhead-valve engines and Chrysler's Hemi-heads were transplanted into anything with wheels. Suspension was upgraded by swapping stock components for heavier-duty parts from station wagons or trucks. A lot of creativity went into modifying stamped-steel wheels for greater width and strength as getting performance from the limited range of high-load bias-ply tires available at the time required a deal of engineering instinct.

'Shine was originally shipped by the case in glass Mason jars, but less-fragile plastic one-gallon milk jugs eventually made the process easier. Some drivers installed large stainless-steel containers in their trunk or rear seat area that could be filled and drained quickly. These "tankers" were often fitted with an easy-open valve in the bottom to empty the contents in seconds without stopping, in case of a revenuer roadblock.

Drivers were typically young men hungry for adventure and desperate for income who could outrun police and revenuers on the dangerous curvy roads of the Appalachians—sometimes at speeds up to 100 miles per hour. Many of them worked on their family's farm by day and ran 'shine at night. Road conditions weren't ideal at that time, with gravel making up the majority of the miles, and some fearless smugglers drove portions with their headlights off. At any given time during the immediate post-Prohibition years, there were likely several thousand active ridge runners operating, most making two to three runs weekly. Their modified engines created a bellow that sounded like thunder echoing through the mountains.

MOONSHINE AND NASCAR

Maneuvering a tail-heavy sedan with more than a half-ton of liquid weight was a skill that meant the difference between a successful delivery, jail time, or a fiery, alcohol-fueled crash at the bottom of a mountain. Weight-induced understeer made the curves scary with a full load and dangerous in bad weather. Thus, ridge runners became known for their driving skills.

After World War II, the desire to develop and show off these talents moved many moonshine transporters to enter their cars in races at tracks on the burgeoning National Association for Stock Car Auto Racing Grand National circuit. NASCAR, which began sanctioning stock car races throughout the southeast and other regions in 1948, was a natural magnet for the wild and often eccentric driving styles of these mountain boys. It was a route to make legal money during the day to supplement the illegal income at night.

Three brothers from Alabama—Bob, Fonty, and Tim Flock—had been running 'shine in Georgia for their uncle before joining the NASCAR circuit in '49. Bob and Fonty enjoyed a combined twenty-three wins during their short careers, but it was Tim's forty victories in 187 starts that gave him a place in the record books. Carefree Tim once drove nine races with a pet rhesus monkey named Jocko Flocko

Facing page, **THUNDER ROAD:** Robert Mitchum's 1958 movie instilled moonshine drivers with heroic legend. The ridge-runner cars also inspired many a hot rod and NASCAR racer, as hillbilly moonshine haulers discovered they could run 'shine at night and earn some extra cash racing during the day.

MITCHUM roars down the hottest highway on earth!

THUNDER ROAD

co-starring GENE **BARRY** · Jacques **AUBUCHON** · with KEELY **SMITH** · TREVOR **BARDETTE** and introducing SANDRA **KNIGHT** · JIM **MITCHUM**

Screenplay by JAMES ATLEE PHILLIPS and WALTER WISE · Based on an original story by ROBERT MITCHUM

Directed by ARTHUR RIPLEY · A DRM Production · Released thru UNITED **UA** ARTISTS

RUTHERFORD COUNTY SHERIFF'S DEPT. MURFREESBORO, TN
SEPT. 30, 1950
L to R - Robert Goodwin, Sheriff George Sharp, seated, Leonard Hill, Grady Haley, John D. Sanford

as his co-driver; Tim lost their final event together when Jocko got loose in the car, forcing an untimely pitstop.

Curtis Turner was a star from NASCAR's earliest days, and his legend includes unverified stories that he was a former moonshine runner. Whether he transported booze or not, Turner certainly consumed enough of it; he was a party animal who could drink and chase women all night before getting in a car and driving to one of his 360 career victories. A Virginia lumberman who never slowed down in life, Turner used one of his fortunes to build Charlotte Motor Speedway in 1960 with Bruton Smith. As a private pilot, Turner once landed his small plane on Charlotte's backstretch without warning. He died in 1970 when he crashed that plane into a mountain in Pennsylvania.

Perhaps the most famous of the early bootlegging racers was Robert Glenn "Junior" Johnson of North Carolina, whose sophomore year in NASCAR's Grand National series was put on hold while he served eleven months in a federal prison after a raid on his family's still. Johnson had a reputation

for using his brain to outrun revenuers. One time, he installed a siren and flashing blue light on his car. He also developed a technique for spinning 180 degrees in the road—without slowing down. He used that same intellectual approach on the racetrack as a competitor before becoming the most successful team owner in NASCAR history when his drivers won six championships in ten years. Ronald Reagan later granted Johnson a presidential pardon, and in 1998 *Sports Illustrated* declared him the greatest NASCAR driver in history.

In the 1960s, NASCAR began a program to move away from its dirttrack roots by developing speedways and superspeedways that greatly increased the base of its fans and the complexity of its race cars. Today, it is the fastest-growing spectator sport in America, but it will never be entirely free of its early moonshine and outlaw influences.

MOONSHINE ON THE SCREEN

In 1958, the movie *Thunder Road* did for southern hot rod culture what *Gone with the Wind* had done for the Civil War, infusing moonshining with a romantic legend of hotted-up cars. Robert Mitchum's pet project started out as a story he conceived about the fictional Doolin clan in Appalachia and its attempt to make an honest living despite the best efforts of the federal government and a powerful crime syndicate.

Mitchum not only wrote the original story, but starred as tragic anti-hero Luke Doolin (with his real-life son James playing his younger brother in a stiff manner that makes Pinocchio seem relaxed by comparison) and co-wrote the movie's title song "Ballad of Thunder Road," which was popular enough to spend eleven weeks on Billboard's chart when it debuted and another ten weeks in a revival four years later.

Thunder Road's story centered on a poor mountain family's internal struggle (Ma is against her boys' hauling hooch from Pa's still) and external conflicts (the hill folk against the feds and syndicate). The film might have been just another low-budget offering for the then-popular "hick pic" and "G-man" genres had it not been for Mitchum's insistence that the specialized transport cars and chases be depicted with authentic detail. The descriptions of the modified equipment, the maintenance given the powerplants and chassis after every illegal run, and the rich dialogue about methods of operation lend the film a verisimilitude missing from other attempts to tell the moonshining story.

Had Mitchum not been such a strong screen presence, he might have played second chair to the hot rod Fords immortalized in the movie. During the film's exposition, Doolin's car is a dark '50 Ford two-door with which he outruns federal agents in a '57 Chevy four-door. When next we see the Ford, it has been resprayed a light gray in order to make identification by the cops more difficult. During the course of the story, Doolin retires his '50, giving it to a fellow ridge runner. He then switches to a '57 Ford two-door, which a dealer in Illinois promised him was "good for 130 on the straights."

FROM RIDGE RUNNERS TO HOT RODS

While young people on the West Coast had long been building their rides to resemble the lightened cars being raced on nearby dry lake beds, *Thunder Road* set the tone for late-model hot rod fashion in the southeastern United States for the next decade or more.

In the South, where most car enthusiasts have seen the movie *Thunder Road* at least a dozen times or more, the '50 and '57 Fords Robert Mitchum drove are as recognizable and desirable as the red Torino from *Starsky & Hutch* or the yellow Mustang from *Gone in 60 Seconds*. A real fan of the movie can't see one of these Fords without humming "The Ballad of Thunder Road"; it's a Pavlovian response similar to what the rest of the world has when spotting a silver Aston Martin DB5 like Sean Connery drove as James Bond in *Goldfinger*.

David Miller's parents made the mistake of taking him to see *Thunder Road* for his first-ever visit to a drive-in theater when he was a young lad in rural Charlotte, North Carolina. Miller figures his lifelong interest in high-performance cars began just a few minutes after the start of the movie, but it would be another thirty-five years before he was able to start building a Luke Doolin–style hot rod.

In 1993, Miller and his wife Judy found a '49 Ford (identical in most outward respects to the '50) in Mount Pleasant, South Carolina. Miller's goal was to create a modern take on the legendary moonshine haulers, a retro car that was comfortable enough to drive every day but powerful enough to give the Duke Boys' General Lee Dodge Charger a run for its money. Their car would be a rolling tribute to the Carolinas' outlaw lore.

Miller and his wife completely disassembled the car as they planned their modifications, and they spent the next three years putting it back together. Under the hood went a Ford 302-cubic inch V-8 with twin four-barrel carburetors and high-performance exhaust headers. Chrome and polished aluminum were tastefully applied to various underhood parts, including the air cleaner housing and valve covers. In order to upgrade the Ford's handling, the Millers installed independent front suspension components from a Mustang II, a rear axle from a Maverick, and five-spoke chromed wheels wrapped by high-performance Goodrich radial T/A tires.

They redesigned the car's interior with a '51 Ford dash; comfortable, leather-covered bucket seats; and a beautiful carmen red-and-white trim—a color scheme that was carried through to the upholstered trunk.

THE GLORIES OF MOONSHINE

Body modifications included a frenched antenna, a hood with dozens of air-breathing louvers, and a concealed fuel cap. Layers of smooth '95 Ford wild-strawberry paint were applied to the body, making Miller's "Moonshiner" nicer than any car the Doolin family ever hauled hooch in.

Cammie Moose is another Carolina native whose automotive life was affected–although indirectly through her father–by *Thunder Road* and its sinister hot rods. Moose always wanted a black-and-white '57 Ford two-door like the one her father owned when she was young. For unknown reasons, he sold the car in 1988 rather than offer it to her–probably hoping to keep the Ford's hopped-up 390-cubic inch V-8 from turning his child into a speed demon.

Just before her father passed away eight years ago, Moose and her husband Billy came across just such a car at a show in Charlotte and bought it. She drove the '57 for a year before Billy took it apart and began serious restoration work.

Billy, who has built race engines for NASCAR Winston Cup drivers Darrell Waltrip, Neil Bonnett, Michael Waltrip, and Harry Gant, mounted the entire Ford body on a giant chassis rotisserie to have access to every nook and cranny. Nine months later, the two-door sedan emerged from the shop the spitting image of Moose's father's car.

Under the '57's gleaming black hood, the engine compartment is as smooth and mirror-like as the rest of the sedan. The car is motivated by a balanced-and-blueprinted 351-cubic inch, 300-horsepower V-8 with valve covers, air cleaner, and various other bits liberally coated in chrome. Billy wanted to install one of Ford's Toploader manual four-speed transmissions behind his stout powerplant, but Cammie asked that the car keep its shifter on the column so it would be similar to her father's old car. It took Billy a while to convert the original "three-on-the-tree" to a four-speed, but the Mooses have a vehicle no ordinary thief could drive away; backing up now requires pulling a knob on the dash. That's a trick any moonshiner would appreciate.

MODERN-DAY MOON-SHINE HAULER:
This '49 Ford coupe was a modern take on the legendary '50 piloted by Robert Mitchum in *Thunder Road.* Power came from a Ford 302-cubic-inch V-8 with twin four-barrel carburetors and high-performance exhaust headers—ideal for outrunning the T-men. (Photographs © Brad Bowling)

THUNDER IN THE HILLS: Getting down to business in his battle with the Feds in *Thunder Road,* Robert Mitchum traded in his '50 Ford for a hotter '57 Ford. This '57 two-door was built as a replica of Mitchum's machine. It was propelled by a 351-cubic-inch, 300-horsepower V-8. (Photographs © Brad Bowling)

The interior is a tasteful blend of old and new. Ford's original dash design has been enhanced with billet aluminum air vents and a CD player. Door panels reflect the chrome-strip layout and styling of the car's exterior, and the seats are original Ford issue, with the exception of one seatbelt for the occasional grandchild passenger. Because Cammie is not the tallest person to ever pilot a '57 Ford, Billy shortened the original steering wheel's diameter to create better visibility. Air conditioning, power steering, and power brakes are some of the creature comforts that found their way into the Ford during its restoration.

Knowing that black paint shows every little imperfection in the body, the Mooses made sure the Ford's fenders, doors, hood, and trunk were laser straight before the dark coats were applied. Billy, whose street-rod-building résumé boasts a dozen or so cars, spent many hours polishing every strip of chrome before re-attaching everything to the perfect sheetmetal.

While the Ford performs like a modern muscle car, the sedan's stock appearance doesn't offer many clues as to its high-speed nature. Only the fat BF Goodrich tires and billet aluminum Renegade wheels give away the secret.

DELINQUENCY

Buzz Gunderson (Corey Allen):
"You know how to chicky-race don't you?"

Jim Stark (James Dean):
"Yeah, it's all I ever do."

—Rebel without a Cause, 1955

DAREDEVILRY AND DELINQUENCY: Other than the distant dry lakes, there were no safe, legal places to race rods in Southern California until after 1950. So these two Model A roadsters duked it out in 1938 down Slauson Avenue in the heart of Los Angeles. (Pat Ganahl collection)

A23

A NOVEL

Speed...Danger
...DEATH!

HOT ROD

HENRY GREGOR FELSEN

"SHOCKING ...
TRUE-TO-FACT"
N.Y. Times

Complete and Unabridged

BUD CRAYNE, Boy Hot Rodder

By Henry Gregor Felsen

Henry Gregor Felsen was the undisputed poet laureate of the hot rod. He was born in Brooklyn, about as far from the center of hot rodding as could be. Instead of cars, Felsen dreamed of writing, but while living in Iowa and after spotting his first hot rods, he was inspired.

He published his novel *Hot Rod* in 1950, winning praise from the august *New York Times,* which called the book "shocking . . . true-to-fact." Hot rodders and teenaged hot-rodding wannabes took up the book and read it with gusto. Felsen told the story right: the female love interest was secondary; the cars came first and foremost. There were lustful descriptions of the mechanicals and thrilling tales of drag races—just what the audience wanted. *Hot Rod* was *The Catcher in the Rye* for the fast set.

After writing some sixty books, Felsen died in 1995, at the age of seventy-eight.

This excerpt from *Hot Rod* encompasses the book's first nine pages, introducing Bud Crayne and his hop-up during their famous run into Avondale, Iowa.

HOT ROD: "Speed . . . Danger . . . DEATH!" promised this classic juvenile-delinquency exploitation cover from the paperback edition of Henry Gregor Felsen's classic novel. The august *New York Times* even branded the book "true-to-fact"—although what they knew about hot rodding in far-off Gotham was difficult to guess.

Bud Crayne rounded a curve at fifty and faced into the setting sun. For the next ten miles the highway ran straight and level across open farm land. Ninety-nine out of a hundred drivers rounded that curve and coming on the flat immediately increased their speed. Bud held at fifty. He had his reasons for staying at fifty. Bud always had a reason for driving at a particular speed.

A new green Plymouth sedan came up fast behind Bud, honked imperiously and swept by. Bud glanced at the other driver as the Plymouth moved past and saw contempt in his eyes for the ancient-looking contraption Bud was driving. Bud watched the new car pull ahead and cut back in front of him, gaining speed and space. He estimated it was hitting seventy, and could tell it was working hard. He laughed to himself but he hated to be passed, even when he wasn't racing.

Fifty. The dual pipes were crooning throatily, the mill was turning like a charm. Bud looked in his rear-vision mirror, made sure the road ahead was clear, then swiftly checked his instrument panel. He noted and remembered the readings of a dozen quivering needles at a glance. Taking a pencil from behind his ear he jotted the readings on a pad strapped to his right leg. That was all for fifty. He stabbed the gas pedal with a gentle toe and his rod leaped to sixty. An easy, effortless sixty. A true sixty.

A short run and an instrument check at sixty. Then seventy. At seventy the dual pipes sang deeper, their rich powerful tones rolling back over the concrete road. At seventy the motor was happy, taking a full bite. Everything checked at seventy. A deeper stab sent the speedometer needle to eighty, and the rpm on the tachometer climbed.

The Plymouth came into view. Whatever its speedometer read, it wasn't grossing more than seventy or seventy-five. Bud's figures for eighty were on the pad.

He wanted ninety, and the Plymouth was in his way. He moved slightly to the left and saw that the road was clear. He gave the Plymouth the horn, waited for the new car to wobble as the driver was startled, then moved to pass. Bud didn't look over to see the other driver's reaction. He didn't care about the other driver. He was interested in making his check at ninety, and that was no speed to rubber-neck at.

As Bud started past the Plymouth the driver of the new car looked to his left to see who was passing him at this speed, expecting to see some more powerful new car. When he saw Bud's crude-looking, home-made job matching wheels with him he almost ran off the road. Not willing to be passed by a car that looked as though it would fall apart at forty, the Plymouth driver tried to make a race out of it. Bud took him on.

For a minute the two cars raced down the highway side by side and only inches apart. As the Plymouth picked up speed Bud stayed with it, until he saw that it was running wide open. Then he opened up. Despite the speed at which he was traveling, he could feel his rear wheels dig the road as he gunned the motor. His car shot ahead and pulled away from the new car, gaining space with every second. The driver of the Plymouth saw it was useless to chase Bud and dropped back to a chagrined and disgusted sixty. He felt disgraced at having been out-run by Bud's stripped-down car, but he was judging from outward appearance alone.

It was a Jacob's coat of a car that Bud Crayne had built. The body had come off an old Ford coupe. Bud had sanded the original black finish and repainted with a dull red prime coat. Some day he intended to put on a finish coat. Bud had also chopped three inches from the top of the body, streamlined the

windshield, and added fenders from another Ford.

He had installed a dropped and filled front axle and cut the frame at the rear to lower the car another three inches closer to the road. As a result, his car looked as though every spring had been broken.

The dual chrome exhaust pipes gave the first hint as to what might be found under the dull red hood. The motor had been taken from a wrecked Mercury, rebored, equipped with a three-carburetor manifold, double springing ignition, re-ground ¾-race camshaft, high compression head, and a score of other refinements and improvements devoted to speed and power.

In contrast to the usual greasy motors found under gleaming hoods, the nondescript body of Bud's car concealed a motor that shone like a warship's brightwork on inspection day. There was chrome wherever chrome could be used. The head, the acorn head nuts, hose connections, exhaust headers, pipes, filters, carbs and linkage system were all of chrome and spotless.

Inside the chopped stubby cab Bud sat behind a huge white steering wheel which, with the side-shifting assembly, had been taken from a Lincoln. The cab was upholstered in artificial red leather with a chrome dash and chrome instruments and knobs. The entire ensemble rode on an ancient Ford chassis with a newer Ford rear end. How all these odds and ends had been fitted together to make one car was the result of months of study, experimenting and hard work on the part of Bud Crayne. It had all been done in his spare time while working at the Avondale Garage and Service Station.

Ninety. Bud traveled the straight highway like a bullet, his pipes blatting against the hard road with the sound of a track racer. At ninety the road seemed to shrink to the width of his wheels, and when he went over small dips in the pavement his car seemed to be dancing lightly on its toes, ready to leap into the air.

Bud leaned forward, listening intently. He didn't like the way the motor was pulling at ninety. Now that his chrome mill was being pushed, it was working too hard for the power and speed it delivered. He pushed on the gas pedal, and altho he was rewarded with more speed the response was soggy. He pushed a little harder, almost all the way, and as he touched one hundred his motor faltered. Bud held at a hundred, listening. Better to figure out the trouble now and fix it, than find out later, when every ounce counted.

At a hundred his rod had a tendency to float, and he had to fight the wheel when he ran into sudden changes in the wind. A black dot coming out of the sun swelled up to a big tractor and trailer. There was no time to cut his speed as they passed. The noise of their passing was like a grenade exploding, and the backwash from the truck hit Bud like a solid blow. His car shuddered from the impact and pulled like a balky horse fighting the bit. Bud fought it through,

SCALLOPED: The 1980s witnessed a revival of real hot rods—the classic 1940s and 1950s rides. This 1980s re-creation of a fifties-style Deuce five-window coupe was pure tradition, even riding on big and little wide whites. In a tip of the hat to engineering advances, it was powered not by a vintage Flathead but by a small-block Chevy breathing through six two-barrels. (Photograph © Pat Ganahl)

but he was forced to the right of the road, and for a moment it felt as though his wheels were going to slide off the pavement and ditch him. He gave it everything and played for the middle of the road. He came out rocking and cut his speed, thankful there was plenty of room and no traffic.

Bud hadn't failed to note the details of engine performance in his burst of speed. He wrote them down on the pad strapped to his leg, then put the pad in the glove compartment. He looked at his watch and saw it was time to head for Avondale and work. He yawned. It had been a fairly dull run on the highway.

Knowing how his car deceived by its looks, Bud liked to patrol that ten mile stretch of straight road. Whenever he could, he teased big cars into racing with him, and usually won. Sometimes he won because his car was faster, but when some unusually fast stock car could approach his speed, Bud counted on his superior driving ability and his nerve to beat down the opposing driver. Most drivers quit easily at high speeds. Not Bud. He liked to win.

On this late afternoon he had gone out primarily to check the performance of his rod, and the Plymouth hadn't given him much of a race. Now that he was headed back to the garage he was ready to tear into his motor and find out where it was weak. There was only one more thing he wanted to try.

Another mile down the road Bud turned north for the two-and-a-quarter mile run into Avondale. The moment he turned off the main highway he was on the stretch of road that all the local drivers regarded as a playground.

The road to Avondale ran straight for a mile. Then it broke to the left in a long, gentle, banked turn that was known as Ninety-Mile-Curve. When the road straightened again, it lay like an arrow for a little over a mile, pointing at the small town. At the end of the flat was an overhead railroad crossing, and the highway coiled into a tight S to go under the tracks. Once around the S and through the underpass, there was Avondale. The entire one unpaved business street of it.

As usual, the Avondale road was deserted. Bud shoved his rod up to ninety by slow stages, so that when he hit Ninety-Mile-Curve he was rolling steadily. Now for the test. He had installed an anti-sway bar and canted his rear springs. That, coupled

with his low center of gravity ought to allow him at least another five. He tried the turn at ninety-five.

It was easy. There was a little pull, but nothing serious. His rod seemed to dig its nose in a furrow and come around without any serious danger of getting out of hand. His tires wailed a little from the side pull, but it was a pleasant sound. He came out of the turn holding a new record, determined to add another five when his mill was in perfect order.

Dropping back to ninety, Bud made a final test for stability. He pointed to the left side of the road, crossed the middle line, then turned back again. As soon as he was on his own side of the road he eased to the left again, and then back to the right. Rocketing, he rocked from right to left, rolling to the fine point where another touch would pull his off wheels from the road. Back and forth across the road he rolled, mightily pleased with the way he could rock and roll without losing control or rolling over. He had the touch. He knew just how much, and how far. It was a wonderful feeling. It was important to know just how far he could push his set of wheels before he made his speed run to Trenton. He thought of mistakes in judgment that would roll him over as purely mechanical problems. It never occurred to him that he might be injured or killed, or that he should be afraid.

Bud cut the gun at the Avondale sign along the highway, went into the S-turn fast, and whipped around it with power on. He burned rubber in a joyful double turn, roared up a slight incline when the turn ended, and another hundred yards on he swung to the right across the gravel approach to the Avondale Garage and Service Station. He eased past the two gas pumps and the service station building

CLUB JACKETS: Hot rod clubs have long identified themselves with car plaques and ever-cool painted leather coats or embroidered cloth jackets, such as these modern-day examples from the Poor Boys and Road Zombies. (Photographs © David Fetherston)

and rolled into the open garage. The run was over. Reluctantly Bud turned off the ignition and climbed out of his car, stretching his arms.

Bud Crayne was a lanky, raw-boned boy of seventeen with a long face, bold, self-confident black eyes, and a thin mouth that almost always held a challenging, reckless smile. He wore an old fedora hat with the brim turned up in front and fastened to the crown with a giant safety pin, a tight fitting black leather motorcycle jacket with zippers in the sides and sleeves and studded with metal buttons, and faded blue denim trousers. On his feet he wore short leather boots ornamented at the ankle with small brass chains.

Bud's parents had died when he was in grade school, and since that time he had lived with a bachelor uncle who shared furnished quarters with his young nephew. At first the housekeeper where they lived had watched over Bud, made sure he wore clean clothes and ate his meals and left for school on time. Bud's uncle didn't know much about taking care of a boy, and let the housekeeper take over. As long as Bud was well and out of trouble, his uncle didn't worry.

During his early years Bud enjoyed an unusual amount of independence. The more he could look after himself, the more he was allowed to. He stayed out late, roamed when and where he wished, and learned a hard kind of self-reliance.

He had started hanging around Jake Clymer's garage almost at once. Jake let him stay, taught him about cars, and paid him for his work. Bud's real interest in cars led him to spend more and more time at Jake's, until, in his teens, he knew everything about cars that Jake could teach him, plus a good deal he'd learned himself out of books and magazines.

Bud had learned to drive while most boys were still struggling with bicycles, and once given this head start behind the wheel, he never relinquished it. He had always been able to out-drive the others, and his leadership behind the wheel was seldom questioned or (any more) challenged.

At seventeen Bud was his own boss, resented any attempts by anyone to guide or counsel (he called it interfering with) his ways, and, he not only worked at Jake's, but practically lived at the garage.

Growing up in this way without a family, Bud always felt different from the other boys and girls in town, and was always a little apart from them. When they turned to the warmth and love in their homes, he, left alone, turned to the garage, and his car. The hours that others spent with mothers, fathers, sisters or brothers, Bud spent with his homemade hop-up. It was his family. He was in the habit—like cowboys who rode lonesome ranges for isolated days at a time and talked to their horses to break the silence—of talking to his car as though it were animate, and could understand, and sympathize.

His independence made him seem more mature than the other boys his age who yet had to ask parental permission to come and go. Bud regarded himself a man, and thought (he thought) like a man. He had a job, and as soon as he was graduated from high school, he was going to be Jake's partner in the garage. Content with this future which assured him an income and a chance to experiment with motors, he considered himself old enough to marry. When high school was over with, and he was working full time, he intended marrying LaVerne Shuler. Why not? He could support a wife, and, for the first time in his life, he would have a real home of his own.

Meanwhile, Bud worked for Jake in his free time. When he wasn't working he was on the road. He tinkered with his car for hours in order to have pleasant moments of speed on the highway. When he was behind the wheel, in control of his hopped-up motor, he was king of the road. When he was happy, his happiness reached its peak when he could express it in terms of speed and roaring power, the pull of his engine, the whistle of the wind in his ears, and the glorious sensation of free flight.

When he was unhappy, discontented, moody, the wheel again offered him his answer. At these times there was solace and forgetfulness behind the wheel. The motor snarled rather than sang, speed became a lance rather than a banner, and revenge against trouble was won through the conquest of other cars that accepted his challenge to race. And when he was alone on the road, his car and its speed seemed to remove him from the troubles that plagued him while his feet had contact with the earth. Once removed from bodily contact with the ground, once in motion, once in a world of his own making, he escaped his troubles and sorrows in speed, in the true touch of the wheel, in the trustworthy thunder of the motor, the rushing sensation of detachment from all that was rooted or planted in earth.

LUCKY LADY: Al Cole owned this '32 coupe for a number of years before he slowly began changing its style from a full-fendered resto-rod to a fenderless Hi-Boy and eventually down to what he really wanted—a fenderless, primered, channeled coupe. The conversion included boxing the stock chassis and adding new X-members with the rear end secured with ladder bars, coil-overs, and a 9-inch Ford axle. The front now rolls on a four-link Speedway Motors front end with a Ford axle and '40 Ford spindles. Buddies Mike Preston, Gunar Hansken, and Ralph Finley helped with the channeling of the body over the frame and with the installation of the refreshed 307 Chevy topped with a tri-pack of Rochester 2G carbs. The body was shot with Krylon flat black spray cans and then Ralph Finely painted the Von Dutch-style "Lucky Lady" to the cowl. Al added some color highlights with gloss red 15-inch Ford steelies. The interior follows the fifties theme to the mark with red pleated Naugahyde trimmed-in by Larry's Custom Upholstery. (Photograph © David Fetherston)

No matter what his mood or his feeling, his trouble or his joy, it made everything right and good to be guiding his car, the car he had built, that belonged to him, that owed everything it was to him. Not a day passed without Bud's taking time for a spin. It was more than a ride; it was more than speeding; more than killing time. In some ways these daily sessions on the road were his hours of meditation, of true self-expression, the balm for his soul and the boast of his spirit. In these flying hours he had sought himself out, molded himself into what he was, and found his creed.

Bud's car, variously called his baby, hop-up, strip-down, roadster, heap, hot rod, jalopy or set of wheels, was like Bud himself. In a way he had built a mechanical representation of his life, and its oddly-assorted parts could be likened to his patch-work past.

Bud had started out in life as the son of two parents. Each part of his car had likewise begun life in a normal automotive way. Then had come death in his family. From a normal home he had been thrust into an abnormal situation, and the product of parents was modified by the care of an uncle, and a strange housekeeper. From the wreckage of normal cars Bud had salvaged a part here and a part there, and assembled them, and modified them so they would fit.

Many people had helped design Bud's development. His parents, his uncle, the housekeeper, Jake, his friends, his teachers. He had been influenced by many sources as he grew, and not all the influences were compatible with one another. Yet each had had some effect on his character, and formed him into what he was, a composite person, belonging neither here nor there, and knowing no twin.

So was his car. From the wrecks and abandoned hulks Bud had taken a Ford piece here, a Lincoln piece there, a Cadillac piece somewhere else, reconciled their differences into one body, added something of his own, and created an automobile that was at once similar to and different from all other automobiles. It lived on the same food and obeyed

STREET RACE: Two street rod coupes get ready to punch off on a backroad near Sacramento. The flamed black coupe features Shotgun Ford power. The red challenger boasts a big-block Chevy. (Photograph © Pat Ganahl)

the same laws, but, like Bud, it had no twin. They were both a little different, a little apart, constructed partly by design and partly by accident, made of the materials at hand, formed, as it were, by-guess-and-by-gosh.

No wonder then that Bud felt more than a pride of ownership in this fellow-hybrid that was his car. Made with the work of his hands and the thought of his brains, it was his totem, his companion, his dog, his drawer of shells, his treasured childhood blanket and fuzzy bear.

Together they were a team, Bud's car and himself. Together they had won local fame and leadership on the road and in the shop. And other boys who worshipped speed came to kneel before this stubby, squat, misshapen little god of speed, and to listen raptly to Bud, the coveralled high priest of the cult. He held chrome engine parts before their eyes, sermonized on gear ratios, chanted of "gow" and "dig" and "drag," and blessed them with a benediction in the form of advice on how to run away from police cars.

EDWARD DE ROO, *GO, MAN, GO!,* 1959: *Go, Man, Go!* was pure hot rod noir. The tone was tough, with hard-boiled violence and graphic sex aimed at a hard-edged teen exploitation market. The cover illustration said it all for what was inside.

HENRY GREGOR FELSEN, *STREET ROD*, 1953: Felsen was the poet of the hot rod, and his numerous novels became beloved chronicles of a hot rodding youth and times gone by. He dedicated *Street Rod* to his buddies in the Iowa Timing Association.

Hot Rod Literature 101

High schools never offered the class. Colleges turned up their noses at it. Universities simply scoffed.

They all should have been paying more attention.

Hot rod literature was hot stuff throughout the 1950s and 1960s. While bored teens were browbeaten into reading "true" literature in English classes, many were secretly thrilling to the exploits of one Bud Crayne, boy hot rodder and the star of Henry Gregor Felsen's multimillion seller *Hot Rod*. It was the best of the best, but just the front runner in a big field racing for readers.

Hot rodding sparked a whole genre of fiction, some titles aimed at teenagers, others written for those wanting a titillating view of the perceived horrors of juvenile delinquency. Either way, it was high-octane stuff.

Henry Gregor Felsen became hot rodding's poet. He published his novel *Hot Rod* in 1950, and the book became an instant classic among hot rodders. Teenagers, dreaming of hopped-up speed and its exhilaration, slipped their copy of the novel behind high-school textbooks and suddenly appeared inspired scholars.

Felsen proved prolific. He followed *Hot Rod* with more odes to cars—*Street Rod*, *Crash Club*, *Rag Top*, *Road Rocket*. His stock-car-racing book *Fever Heat*, written under the pen name Angus Vicker,

ROBERT SIDNEY BOWEN, *HOT ROD ANGELS*, **1960, AND** *HOT ROD FURY*, **1963:** Bowen wrote a long series of juvenile hot rodding novels aimed at the readership spawned by Henry Gregor Felsen's *Hot Rod*.

hit the silver screen in 1968. Felsen had become the Hemingway of Dead Man's Curve, and his fans couldn't get enough.

One of the most published hot rod authors was Robert Sidney Bowen, a talented writer better acquainted with a typewriter than a monkey wrench. Bowen didn't build hot rods, but he certainly could tell a tale. At age fourteen, he lied about his age, flew as a pilot in World War I, and became an ace. Hankering for adventure during the ensuing peace, he wrote for the legions of pulp magazines and radio serial shows, dreaming up thrilling stories that kept readers and listeners on the edges of their seats.

In 1960, Bowen published *Hot Rod Angels* and found an appreciative new audience among the car crowd. Like the hot rod movies of the day, it was simple stuff, automotive morality tales in which kids learn the hard way not to race in the streets. But it rang true, and readers avidly bought his following books—*Hot Rod Inferno*, *Hot Rod Fury*, *Hot Rod Doom*, *Hot Rod Rogues*, and more.

While Felsen's *Hot Rod* was indisputably the masterpiece of the genre, the dark horse in the field was a novel titled *Go, Man, Go!* by Edward De Roo. De Roo was another pulp writer in the vein of Raymond Chandler, Dashiell Hammett, and Horace McCoy, and he penned such juvenile-delinquent "exploita-

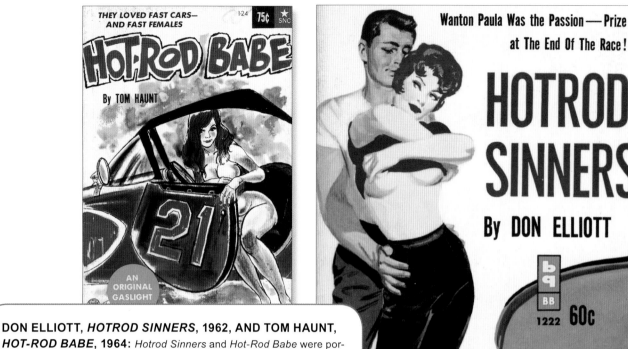

DON ELLIOTT, *HOTROD SINNERS*, 1962, AND TOM HAUNT, *HOT-ROD BABE*, 1964: *Hotrod Sinners* and *Hot-Rod Babe* were pornography for those with hot rodding second on the mind. And in fact, these were the same books, with just the heroine's name changed from Paula to Jayne—presumably to protect the innocent.

CHARLES VERNE, *MR. HOT ROD*, 1957: Just as the cover depicted, there were more descriptions of girls than of hot rods in this steamy novel.

tion" novels as *Rumble at the Housing Project*, *The Young Wolves*, *The Little Caesars*, and *The Fires of Youth*—racy books packed with sex and violence.

Go, Man, Go! was a hot rod coming-of-age story like no other. It told the tale of Paul Sanders, an upstanding newspaper boy with the usual dreams of cars and girls. But Sanders runs afoul of everyone, stealing the girlfriends of the hot rod gang leader and

his best friend, getting caught between his father and the law, and living for horsepower. The writing was taut, the prose hard-boiled, the mood pure noir. It was a classic of its kind.

You likely read these books, hidden behind serious literature during English class or by flashlight underneath the bedcovers at night. If not, it's never too late to start. —Michael Dregni

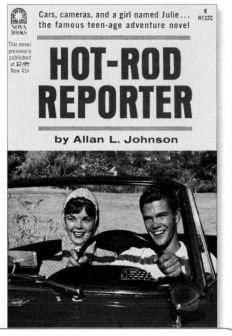

Cars, cameras, and a girl named Julie... the famous teen-age adventure novel

K
N132C

NOVA BOOKS

This novel previously published at $2.95 Now 45¢

HOT-ROD REPORTER

by Allan L. Johnson

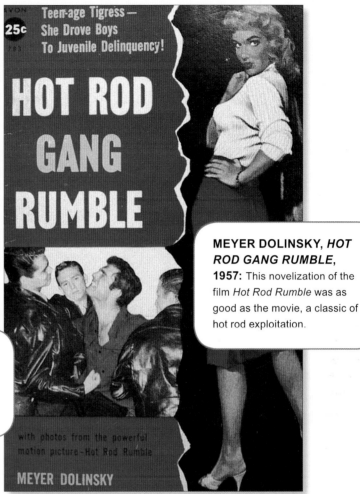

Teen-age Tigress — She Drove Boys To Juvenile Delinquency!

25¢

HOT ROD GANG RUMBLE

with photos from the powerful motion picture—Hot Rod Rumble

MEYER DOLINSKY

MEYER DOLINSKY, *HOT ROD GANG RUMBLE*, 1957: This novelization of the film *Hot Rod Rumble* was as good as the movie, a classic of hot rod exploitation.

ALLAN L. JOHNSON, *HOT-ROD REPORTER*, 1965: Cub reporter Mark Williams was on his way to the big time if he could only reconcile his newspaper job with hot rods and a girl named Julie. As the cover showed, everything turned out rosy.

POPULAR LIBRARY 25¢ He Liked Fast Cars And Beautiful Women

656

PASSION ROAD

RICHARD GLENDINNING
Author of "TOO FAST WE LIVE"

Complete and unabridged

Left, **RICHARD GLENDINNING, *PASSION ROAD*, 1955:** *Passion Road* was pure pot-boiler, packed with tales of racing hot rods in the Carrera Panamericana, fiery crashes, fiery romance, and boring clichés.

ACE DOUBLE BOOKS

DAYS AND NIGHTS OF A JUVENILE DELINQUENT

D-214

HATE ALLEY

35¢

MARTIN L. WEISS
Complete Novel

MARTIN L. WEISS, *HATE ALLEY*, 1957: The author was touted as a former Los Angeles County sheriff with firsthand insight into the ways of hot rodding juvenile delinquents. This exposé was less concerned with their cars, however, than describing in overly delicious detail the JDs' fates.

A PORTRAIT OF THE ARTIST
as a Young **Hot Rodder**

By Robert Williams

Robert Williams is hot rodding's Picasso—or perhaps more correctly, its Salvador Dali. He lists as his artistic muses influences ranging from classic and modern academic art to carnival midway banners, pulp magazine covers, underground comix, hot rod T-shirt art, and the like. Williams describes his own artwork in his book *Visual Addiction* as "silly to the point of atrocity—catastrophically zany." He doesn't just draw nice pictures of nice cars; Williams' paintings themselves are hot-rodded art.

Williams is of course also a hot rodder himself, with roots stretching back decades. This remembrance of things past was told to Pat Ganahl and first appeared in *Rodder's Journal*.

FLAMES: Candy Apple Green flames grace the hood of this metallic purple machine. (Photograph © David Fetherston)

STORY NO. 1

It was 1959 and I was in high school in Albuquerque. This kid used to come to school in this hot rod. It was a '30 Model A coupe; the body was channeled; Model A engine; the radiator was still sitting up real high; maybe it had hydraulic brakes. He took the headlight bar and bent it in shop class for headlight mounts, but when he put 'em on, the tires hit, so he reversed them, so the headlights sat real close together (laughs). Picture this thing—with a stock-height radiator, headlights right next to each other, channeled body, no firewall, no windshield, and no windows. And he's sitting on a piece of plywood.

He comes by my house one day. I was working on a '27 T roadster in my garage. And he wants me to go riding with him somewhere. So I get in this coupe; we're sitting on a piece of plywood—maybe some pillows. And there's the engine, and the transmission, and the street. No windshield in this thing. And we go cutting down the street in it. It's pretty fast. The street makes a T at the end, and he's got this thing wide open. I figure he's going one way, but he throws it into a brodie and goes the other way. And when he throws it into a brodie, the body lifts up. He just had some strap mounts or something that were sitting on the frame, without bolts in 'em. So the body lifts up on his side, and I see daylight. The body goes over and hits the wheelwell on the tire (sound effects), and this causes the car to start swerving. So he brings it back, and the body comes back down—*ka-chump!*—on

his side, and lifts up on my side! And I'm sitting there looking at the ragged-cut edge of the body, up in the air, and then it comes back down, *wham!* I could have gotten my leg cut off! So he gets it straightened out, but the radiator's still going back and forth, and it falls back into that two-bladed fan, and hot water goes everywhere. There's no windshield or firewall or nothin'. We're almost scalded in this thing! And he says, "Well, I think I better take you home."

I was white as a ghost. I got on him really hard about making some modifications to this thing to make it safer. But he didn't want to hear about it. He just dumped me off at home.

Next thing I know, he's got in with some other hot rod friends, and he's put a brand new 348 and a four-speed in this thing, with a Chevy rear end. The rest of the car is still exactly like I described it to you—the high radiator, the headlights together. The top was open on it. He had six two's on this thing. It was a meteorite. He took me for a ride in it, and I says, "Look, I'm not going to get in this thing again with that cowl gas tank. If something goes wrong with the clutch or something . . . or those carburetors light off . . ." And the carburetors always did light off, that was the thing. If you've got six carburetors and you're not a good mechanic, your valley is continually full of gasoline. He'd start this thing, and it'd backfire and ignite the whole valley in fire, but then he'd go *whomp, whomp* with the gas pedal and suck all the fire down the carburetors.

He had some friends who did some good work to get the rear end installed, and the motor mounts installed—that was done fairly efficiently. But other than that, it was nothin', just like it was before.

So one day he comes by, and he says he doesn't have that cowl tank anymore. "I put the tank in the back." So we went driving around. It was really fun to ride around in. It hauled ass!

We went to the filling station to get gas. He opens the trunk so the attendant can fill it, and he's got this wrecking-yard gas tank back there, and it's got bricks and two-by-fours holding it in place. I forget what happened, the attendant jiggled it or something . . . there was some disturbance back there. Anyway, after it's gassed up, he starts it, the flames jump way up, he hits the throttle and sucks 'em down the carbs—the attendant's eyes are like saucers! So he takes off out of there, and sets it into a brodie on Central Avenue, and I hear something go *BA-BAM!* The gas tank fell out, right on the street.

STORY NO. 2

The car clubs in town were kind of wimpy, so I didn't want to have much to do with them. They were mostly guys with new cars with different hubcaps. Then I lost my garage, so I had to join a club, so I joined the Rickshaws—a club that had a giant facility. The Rickshaws was kind of an underground group. They were very productive, running modified race cars and dragsters. They were advanced hot rodders—they had people on the cover of *Hot Rod Magazine.*

I had a '27 T roadster with two feet chopped out of the turtledeck. It sat on Model A rails. The body was moved back and dumped on the frame—it was channeled nine inches at the firewall and stock height at the back. It had a '56 Olds engine, a Deuce grille shell, a V8-60 tube front axle, F100 wheels, and a Halibrand quick-change. With the back end sticking up like that, Pontiac taillights and the Halibrand quick-change, it really stood out. A real classic little roadster.

We used to get a truck and a trailer, and we'd go all through the Southwest—this was the late '50s—and we'd collect all this T stuff from people's farms. A, Deuce, and T stuff; a little bit of '34 stuff. We brought back a ton of it. I had a stack of '23 roadster bodies in my garage all the way to the roof!

I was totally into hot rodding. Too much so. That's why I had to back off a little when I came out to California. See, the problem was that in the '50s, there were people that were, like, really square, and then there were people that were really interesting

PRIME RODS: Artist Robert Williams grew up with hot rods and is still an active rodder today. His "Eights & Aces" Deuce roadster was one of the first modern primer rods, inspiring the rat rodders of today. His wife Suzanne's much-chopped '34 sedan still runs in gray prime. (Photograph © Pat Ganahl)

that were criminals. There was no in-between. If you had imagination, and you were interested in things, you tended to go with these criminal people. 'Cause the others were into sports, and school; they were high-minded; they were all identical people . . . who resented me for being a little different. I wasn't a criminal, a bad person, but I was right in there with 'em. There was a lot of stealing going on. But then "stealing" was like a borderline word too. You know, we'd take a truck, and we'd be gone a week, and we'd come back with all this stuff, and almost always we'd get a long-distance phone call from a sheriff saying, "Either bring the stuff back, or make some adjustment with the landowner, or you're going to jail. We got your license number; saw you removing property." So we'd have to make some adjustment; give him fifty bucks or something.

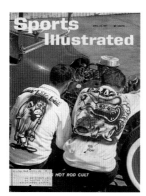

STORY NO. 3

One time my friend Joe and I were in his '34 coupe. It had a 348, no windshield, no brake lights, and who knows what else. It was two in the morning. We'd been drinkin', and we were with two under-age girls—there were four of us in this coupe. And the cops pull us over. Oh shit—violation of curfew . . . they had us for everything but the Mann Act. We figured we were going to do time on this one. The cop comes up: "Joe, I want to talk to you." Joe goes back there.

In that town, everybody knew everybody. When a cop's on you, he's always on you. Anyway, five minutes later Joe comes back and we drive off. So I say, "What the hell was that all about?" Turns out the cop was looking for someone to get him some contraband for an undercover job.

Joe also had a gold '40 Ford coupe, a really nice one.

We were ditching school, and there were four of us in the car. I was in the back on the jump seat. We're driving around, and we're up on Girard Boulevard. It has big grass medians down the middle, about twenty feet wide, with low curbs. It's a big boulevard with nice houses—mansions.

So like an idiot, Joe jumps that curb and drives down the middle, jumps off at the intersection, then jumps back on, jumps off at the next street. We did that all down the boulevard. This is the most fun in the world!

Well, we went and did something else, then came back later, and school had just let out. And here's this school bus full of girls going down Girard. And we're going down that same street in that '40 Ford, and here's this busload of good-lookin' girls, so we're going to do that trick again for them. But this time the city had turned the sprinklers on. We jump on that median, the sprinklers are goin', and the girls are screaming, then we'd jump off the curb. Then we'd jump on it again, do the same thing, and people just flipped. This was a kick in the butt. Well, we did this a couple of times, and then all of a sudden we're stuck. We just sank right down in. The bus drives off, and we're sittin' there. We were stuck for hours! People had seen what we were doing, and nobody was going to give us a hand. Finally, a guy from the city comes by with a truck. He turns the water off and pulls us off with a chain.

About an hour later, we're driving around, and we'd already forgotten about it—we'd had new adventures since then . . . this was just a day in the life—and all of a sudden here come the red lights. We had broken a water main! So they get a police car in front and a police car in back, and we're in this '40 Ford, and they escort us down to the police station. Joe's car was overheating, so they let us park it in back, where the police garage was. They take us in and read the riot act to us. When they're done with that, they let us go out the back door. It's got this porch that's even with the roofs of a whole row of police cars parked in back. So as we leave, we walk the roofs of this whole row of cop cars—right in front of these cops screaming at us.

Then we go across the alley to the police garage to get the '40, and Joe gets the mechanic to solder up his radiator for him. He says, "If I pull this radiator out, will you solder it up for me?" And he gets him to do it. I'm not kidding.

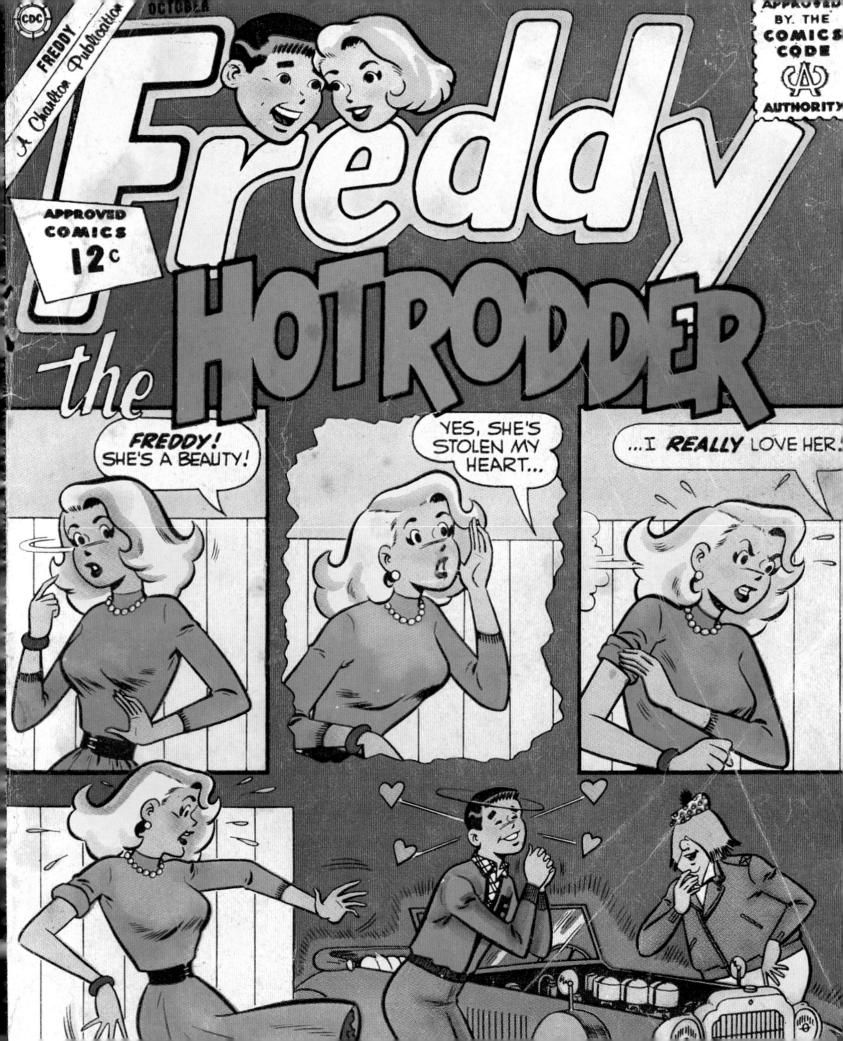

True Confessions

By Henry Highrise

"Henry Highrise" is a hot rodding alias designed to protect the innocent—or at least allow him to share his stories.

Most every hot rodder has a few tales such as these tucked away in his memory that are brought out to regale friends on cruise nights or at show gatherings. Most of us never chicken-raced. Most of us never dueled with out-of-town bad guys and watched them drive over cliffs to meet a fiery demise. Our remembrances are, by and large, good, clean fun—usually spiced with just a bit of daredevilry and delinquency. These are just all-American tales of good times past, the kind of legends that makes hot rodding what it is.

TRUE CONFESSIONS: The truth about the mysteries of love was unveiled in this 1962 Charlton Comics exposé, *Freddy the Hotrodder.*

Throughout the early '60s, I was a true-blue Ford man. I had a '55 Ford powered by a 312 Thunderbird Special with a highrise manifold, four-barrel Holley, and a three-quarter cam. That car got me the nickname Henry Highrise—Henry for the Ford and Highrise for the intake.

Well, before that 312 went in there, I had a stock 292 with a factory four-barrel. I don't remember what make that carb was, we just always called them a Teapot dome. As far as carbs go, they were not worth a flip.

Anyway, there was a guy in the little Oregon town where I lived who had a '56 Chevy 283 Power Pack, and he was beating everyone on the street. I had a rep to protect. I ran that Chevy with my Ford—and got beat. Bad.

I went home and told my dad and it made him good and mad. He was a hot rodder and race mechanic. He worked on my car and speed tuned it and did some tricks to it. Then he told me to go find the guy and beat him. I had a cool dad; my friends' dads were not at all like that—they would have gotten grounded for racing. I looked up the guy in the Chevy and the race was on. I got beat again, just not near as bad.

Well, word traveled around town that my car was not hot anymore. This made my dad furious. My dad had me drive his own car to school for a couple of days while he worked on mine. I don't know what all he did to that Ford, but the next time out that Chevy only had me by half a car-length.

Well, Dad was tore up about it. He told me to take his car and go beat that Chevy. Dad's car was a '58 Ford Custom 300 with a 352 Police Interceptor in it. He had done a backyard port-and-polish job on it and it would fly.

So here we go again, I laid it to that '58 and I beat that Chevy by about one and a half car-lengths. But just after I crossed the finish line, that 352 blew up. Yup, I finally beat the Chevy but blew up the engine in my dad's car doing it.

I didn't want to go home, but my dad was cool: he told me that I blew it up and I was going to rebuild it. With my dad by my side, that was the first engine that I ever rebuilt. I went on to make a career as a master mechanic, and have often thought about this first rebuild. I have built many, many engines since that day.

Well, a new era had started and it was called the small-block Chevrolet. They would run like a banshee stock and were easy to modify to get more horsepower out of them. It was hard for a Ford to stay with them in those days.

327 BREAKFAST OF CHAMPIONS

The small-block Chevys had been around since 1955, and I had my share of trouble beating some of those 283 Power Packs with my '55 Ford. I had my 312 Thunderbird Special bored 0.030 over and put a three-quarter Isky cam in it. After being frustrated with the old Teapot dome carburetor, I replaced the manifold with that highrise and put a big Holley four-barrel on it. My dad did a backyard port-and-polish job on my heads. I decided that the old Ford-A-Matic was not what a rodder needed. So

a trip was made to the junkyard for a swing-pedal assembly, trans, flywheel, and bellhousing, and we changed her over from automatic to standard shift as I put a Foxcraft shifter on the floor. We then went back to the junkyard for a rear end as the automatic's rear end was geared too high for the straight gearbox. A set of homemade traction bars made from schedule 40 black pipe and tie-rod ends went underneath at the same time. Now my hot rod was really hot. I was blowing the 265 and 283 small-block Chevys away.

Then a new small-block came out with 327 cubes. Well, I tracked down the first guy I could find running a 327 and ate his lunch. I beat so many of those 327s that I painted "327 Breakfast of Champions" on the rear deck lid of my car.

I was doing real well beating the Chevys until something new came out. It was called a 30-30 Duntov cam, followed by Crane cams, and on and on. There became so much stuff available to squeeze horses out of 327s that I could not keep in the game with them anymore. You could get speed stuff for the old Ford Y-blocks but the selection was not as great as for the Chevys and the prices were higher. I remember my dad telling me that I could still beat them, but "Speed costs money—how fast do you want to go?"

That spelled the end of that old Ford hot rod of mine. I just loved that old '55 Ford and I wish I still had it.

HILLBILLY HOT ROD

In 1963, my family moved from Oregon to Tupelo, Mississippi. I was in high school, and went drag racing on Friday nights. We started out with a dirt strip and then finally got a paved strip to race on. It was an old crop-duster runway and it ran alongside a big Mississippi cotton field. I don't think the strip was sanctioned in any way and the rules were probably not correct. But we were racing and having fun.

One night some good old boys came down to the strip. They were driving a '58 Ford four-door. The car looked rough. It was covered in mud and had rust holes in it so big you could stick your arm through them. One of the headlights was half full of water. None of the tires matched. There was copper tubing coming out from under the dash and then wrapped around the steering column about three turns; at the end of this tubing was an oil-pressure gauge sticking up behind the steering wheel. With sideburns all the way down to their jaws, these guys looked like they were straight from the hills.

Well, that car looked like a piece of junk, but it would run. Those hillbillies beat everything they were classed with. Then some guys running in other classes wanted to run them. The hillbillies beat everything out there. They got to acting smart and spotting the other cars so many lengths. Nothing could beat them. I figured that hillbilly machine must be an old moonshiner's car or something.

Well, like I said, we just kind of made up our rules as we went. So someone made a protest and put up some money—best I can remember, I think it was a hundred bucks. If these boys wanted to be able to come back to the strip and also keep any money they had won, they had to tear their engine down. If it was what they said it was, they would be in good standing and also get the protest money. If not, they had to pay a hundred bucks and forfeit all their winnings. So they pulled that car into an old aircraft hanger by the side of the dragstrip and tore it down.

I remember a bunch of us staying out there all night long to watch that teardown. The engine turned out to be just what they said it was—a stock 352 Police Interceptor.

Well, to make a long story short, they put that thing back together, and guess what? It ran just like any other '58 Ford after that. So what was the deal? Through the years after that, many theories evolved about why it ran so fast before and not after. Some folk believed it was carbon buildup in the piston tops and combustion chambers increasing compression ratio and that carbon was disturbed or knocked off during the teardown and re-assembly. That's an interesting theory, but I just cannot see getting that much gain from carbon.

This car became a legend around those parts and was talked about for many years afterward. If I had not been there, I would never have believed it. But even today I sure wish I knew the answer, as that baby would fly!

UNLUCKY STRIKE

Back then, we didn't have all of the hot rod stuff we do now. There were only a few companies then that made high-performance camshafts. Back then, our cams were basically still one-quarter, half-quarter, three-quarter, and full race. There also weren't even all the cool racing and hot rod T-shirts that we have now.

I went to the local Drags one night and a guy was set up there selling camshafts, called his company Ed Brown Racing Cams. I had never heard of him before or since. He also had Ed Brown Racing Camshaft T-shirts for sale—you got a free one if you bought a cam. I couldn't afford a cam, but I managed to scrape up enough money to buy a T-shirt. Man, that shirt was my prized possession! It told the world—or so I thought—that I was a real hot rodder. I wore that shirt every chance I got.

One day, that T-shirt wound up on the backseat of my car. I had been out cruising around and on my way home I was cruising down the highway and smoking a Lucky Strike. I casually threw my cigarette out the window and thought nothing more about it.

A couple miles on, I smelled something like electrical wires burning. I was reaching and feeling up under the dash to see if any wires were hot or on fire. I finally looked over my shoulder and that T-shirt and my rear seat cushion were on fire. Guess that Lucky Strike butt blew back in the car.

Well, I'm miles from nowhere, so I pull over on the shoulder and yank the rear cushion out. I had an ice chest in the trunk, so I poured the ice water from it onto the seat cushion. Man, that foam rubber is tough to put out when it's burning. I got it out and started back down the road and I got to smelling that smell again. I looked in the back and sure enough it was burning once more. Pulled over again, yanked the seat cushion out, and slid it under the front of the car and drained about half of my water and antifreeze on it. I finally made it home and water-hosed the dickens out of it.

I was more upset about losing my T-shirt than I was the rear seat cushion—I had my priorities right! I got new padding put in the seat and new seat covers, but I never saw that cam salesman again after that so I couldn't replace my favorite shirt.

And I was always careful with those Lucky Strikes after that.

HIGH JINX

In 1964, I was building a drag car, a '38 Chevy coupe with a 413 Chrysler engine in it. Well, myself and a friend were working on the car one night. The car was far from being finished, but it would run and we decided to take it for a drive. There were no seats in the car yet, so we stacked up two wooden Coca-Cola crates to sit on. We didn't have the gas pedal or linkage on the car yet either, so I tied a piece of bailing wire to the carb and handed my friend the end of the wire and a five-cell flashlight. I told him to shine the light on the road and give it gas with the wire when I said, "Pull!" and to let off when I said, "Let off." My father and I were running a gas station in east Tupelo. The car was in one of the service bays and it was about 11 P.M. when we roared out of that bay.

We were scooting down east Main Street Tupelo in style. We got out of town on a two-lane highway and let her go wide open. Here we were with open headers roaring, five-cell flashlight bobbing up and down, and operating the car with a piece of wire for a throttle.

Well, the Highway Patrol got after us. We had two things going our way—well, maybe three. One, we were faster. Two, the troopers knew the highways and I knew the backroads. Three, we were crazy—if you haven't figured that out yet.

I left the highway and hit the backroads. My friend knew just when to accelerate or decelerate and we got on it, made several turns, and outfoxed that highway patrolman.

We got back into town and hid the car behind the gas station. My Dad saw the car behind the station the next morning and guessed what happened. He and I laughed about that for years.

SURPRISE!

When we moved from Oregon to Mississippi, my '55 Ford did good on the trip until I got within 15 miles of Tupelo, where it gave up and threw a rod. One of my cousins owned the best auto repair business in town, and as I did not have any tools or a place to work on the car, I took it to him. Well, he happened to be a certified speedometer calibration specialist also. As a result he did speedometer work for the Highway Patrol. There were always patrolmen hanging around his shop.

While my cousin was rebuilding my engine, one of the patrolmen noticed the car. You could just tell it was not an adult's car, and he got to asking questions about it. My cousin told him that I was having a port-and-polish job as well as the standard rebuild and was also putting a three-quarter race cam in it. Well, from that day on I think that guy stalked me. It seemed like every other time I looked in the mirror he was behind me. This was nerve-wracking to say the least: he was just waiting for me to step out of line.

One night that patrolman caught me traveling at speed. He turned around and hit the red light (we still had red lights in those days; went to blue a year or so later). I hit the backroads and put the pedal to the metal, made several turns, and again I outfoxed him. I slipped back into town and parked the car behind the house. I let it stay there for a few days and hitched rides to school with a friend.

Now there was this cute blonde girl at school and I finally got up the courage to ask her for a date. Friday night came and I went to pick up my date. I knocked on the door and the door opened—and guess what? It was that same highway patrolman!

He looked me in the eye and then looked past me at my car. I was trying to turn invisible but I didn't know how. He then invited me in and told me not to drive fast with his daughter in the car. He also told me that if I ever pulled anything again like I had done and he caught me, he was going to throw the book at me. I was a marked man. But you know, he and I never had a problem after that and he quit following me around.

Try some of these stunts today and you'll go to jail. But these were good days and good times. Had it made then and did not know it. Good thing the Lord was watching out for me!

CHAPTER 6

CRUISING

He went back to the one place where he knew he belonged, the one place that was his, and his alone—his car.

—Meyer Dolinsky, *Hot Rod Gang Rumble*, 1957

GOLDEN STREAK: Frank Livingston flashes by in his '49 Chevy custom. Inspired by the glorious creations of George and Sam Barris, Frank's ride is a throwback to classic custom days. (Photograph © David Fetherston)

The Saga of SCREAMING MIMI

By Tom Benford

Tom Benford is no stranger to automobiles. He's the author of a variety of car histories and practical guides, from *The Corvette Encyclopedia* to *The Complete Idiot's Guide to Restoring Collector Cars.* Yet sometimes even a car guy gets completely taken by surprise.

Such was the case when Tom and his wife Liz spotted the hot rod they'd come to call Screaming Mimi. Call it what you will—a midlife crisis or just a serious case of automotive lust—but this machine and its bizarre mechanical peculiarities restoked Tom's lifelong passion for cars.

This story is dedicated to the memories of Roy Merkel, Les George, Steve Martin, and Wacky Wayne, who all now do their cruising on the astral plane.

THE SAGA BEGINS . . .
Picnics can wait; working on the hot rod comes first, as shown in this 1954 illustration.

Like every other kid who had attained driving age, I was bitten with the car bug in my teens. Grandiose dreams on a soda-pop budget, however, relegated my first cars to be clunkers barely a breath away from the junkyard. Yet with lots of sweat equity, bartering, and conniving to get the parts and tools I needed, I succeeded in building some hot rods that were real contenders in the local street races.

Fast forward three or four years and now I'm married with one child already here and another one on the way. No place for hot rods in my life now, so the old street racer was sold to make the down payment on a Ford Country Squire station wagon. All dreams of high-performance cars and hot rodding were put on indefinite hold for the next couple of decades.

Now, once the kids were grown and out on their own, my wife Liz and I decided to kick back a bit and start enjoying our old life again. Little did we know that our annual Memorial Day weekend outing to Hyannis, Massachusetts, would rekindle my love affair with cars and that Liz would catch the hot rod bug, big time.

Memorial Day weekend 1995 started out pretty much the way it had in previous years. Liz and I drove up to Cape Cod to escape the throngs of tourists invading the New Jersey shore where we live. As always, the 300-mile ride was pleasant and uneventful.

Upon arrival at the Cape late Friday afternoon, we checked into Tara's Resort, freshened up, and then headed over to Mitchell's Steak House for dinner, all in keeping with past years. The agenda for the next day was to drive over to the Mashpee flea market to wander about in search of unknown treasures.

As we were leaving Hyannis on our way to Mashpee, there sat an outrageous hot rod in the parking lot of a local garage, Ken's Auto Repairs. This car was absolutely wild—a huge engine that looked like it was way too big for the car, no hood, no fenders, and fire-red flames painted along the sides. Standing still this car looked like it was going 100 mph. And it had a "for sale" sign on its windshield.

In previous years as we had passed Ken's Auto Repairs we noticed that he usually had something tasty for sale on his lot. A few years back it was a 1955 Chevy Sedan Delivery, then a '57 Chevy with ladder traction bars, and the previous year a garish pink and purple five-window coupe that I assumed was a '32 Ford from the body style and radiator. Apart from this stick-a-finger-in-your-eye paint job, the car was lackluster, with a small-block motor and chrome reverse wheels. Nothing to write home and tell the kids about, for sure.

The coupe that inhabited Ken's lot now was another story altogether. It was Chrysler Black Cherry with plenty of clear coat on top that made it look like it was under glass. Tuned equal-length headers stuffed into baloney-slashed mufflers took care of the exhaust, while a high-rise tunnel-ram manifold provided a lofty platform for the two four-barrel carburetors upon which a butterfly scoop was mounted.

Liz said, "Boy, look at that. Isn't it wild? Too bad we couldn't register a car like that in New Jersey."

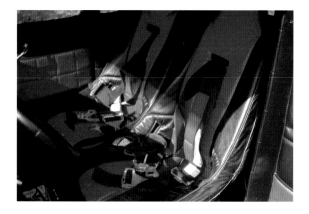

I responded without hesitation, "We could register it as a historic vehicle—it's obviously more than twenty-five years old, so there's no hassle with inspection for it, either. I want to get a closer look at this thing."

With that, we pulled into Ken's parking lot, got out of the car, and started circling around this go-kart-on-steroids like a pair of vultures over a ripe carcass in the desert.

The car had attitude. I think more than anything else, the real appeal was this huge motor overflowing the engine compartment; whoever built this car was apparently a very sick puppy.

And speak of the devil, who should appear but Ken himself from inside the garage. While he was still about thirty feet away, he said, "It's nuts, huh?"

I nodded, and inquired, "What is it? The radiator looks like a '32 Ford, but the body doesn't really look like a Deuce Coupe."

"It's a '33 Dodge," Ken answered as he continued to advance in our direction. "It's got lots of cool stuff; here, check it out," he offered.

With that, he started pointing to the various components of the car and went into an almost Zen-like litany of the features.

"The engine's from a 1972 Chevy Monte Carlo. It's a big-block: 402 cubes, 11:1 domed pistons, Mallory dual point distributor, MSD ignition, 10-degree cam, dual 500-cfm Edelbrock four-barrel carbs on a high-rise aluminum tunnel ram manifold, four-bolt

HUMPY: Al Lindstrom had built hot rods and classics for years, so when it came to building a '37 "Humpy," he knew exactly what he wanted. The frame was redone with a '78 Camaro sub-frame to utilize the independent suspension and disc brakes. It also features Vega steering, a pair of Fat Jack sway bars, and Zenith wheels. The body was prepped and painted by Mike Gray at the Citrus Heights Bodyshop in Sacramento and then finished off by Kirt Strouse with the fiery blue, purple, magenta, and pink flames. A pair of belly pans were fabricated to run under both sides and under the gas tank; then before the car was assembled the chassis was perfectly detailed and painted to match the body. Al installed a '78 350 small-block, which was lightly built with TRW internals and Crane valvetrain. A matching Turbo 350 transmission mates with the V8. The rod was a two-year project, and has since been driven extensively up and down the West Coast, for pleasure and to rod runs and shows. (Photograph © David Fetherston)

mains, balanced and blueprinted . . . ," he continued on and on about the transmission, rear end, interior, and so forth.

Ken confided that he had originally built the car for the dragstrip and ran it for a couple years with a small-block Chevy engine. I inquired if it was ever purple and pink, and he responded that it had been. His reason for selling the car was to raise cash to expand his business, so he decided to repaint the car a more subtle color and install a big-block for sex appeal. Red flames, no fenders, no hood, monster motor with huge headers. Subtle—yeah, right.

I was trying to absorb everything Ken said and analyze it as he continued to rattle off interesting little details about the car. Meanwhile, Liz was checking out the car closely, smiling, and occasionally muttering words to the effect of "Very cool" and "Wow!"

I asked Ken how much he wanted for the car, and he told me a number that had the same effect on my psyche that the car had on my eyes. I told him we

were on our way to Mashpee and that Liz and I would talk it over. He said that was cool. We shook hands and departed.

The eight or so miles to the flea market were dominated by our discussion of this crazy car we had just seen up close and personal. Liz asked if the price Ken was asking was a good one and I, in truth, had no idea if it was or wasn't. I mean, after all, we came up here for a holiday weekend; I certainly never intended to buy a hot rod. At any rate, I told her that I thought the car was worth what he was asking, but it's my nature to haggle, so that's what I intended to do. We wandered around the flea market for about forty-five minutes without buying anything since both of us were still thinking of and talking about that insane little Dodge coupe that looked like a full-size version of a Hot Wheels car.

We again stopped at Ken's place on our return. He came out smiling and said, "I knew you guys would be back."

Not wanting to tip our hands that we really wanted the car, I casually said to Ken, "Well, before I make any decisions I want to go for a test drive."

Ken said, "Sure thing, but I'll drive—this car takes a bit of getting used to and I have my dealer plates on it. Get in on the passenger side and strap yourself in."

"Strap myself in?" I wondered. I just wanted to make sure this thing ran, turned, and stopped OK—what kind of a ride was this guy going to take me on?

Ken pumped the accelerator pedal a couple of times, flicked the "start" toggle switch on and, after the motor was turning over for a couple of seconds, he pushed the "ignition" toggle down and the engine roared to life, creating a ground-shaking din in the process. After letting it warm up for about a minute, he snicked the shifter into drive and we proceeded down a quiet Cape Cod side street.

About a mile down the road, Ken made a "K" turn while explaining that you could simply put the car in drive or "You can romp on it by slapping it through the gears." By the time he said this, we were once again pointed down the straightaway and he briskly slapped the shift handle all the way down to "1." He savagely smashed the accelerator to the floor and as he did the rear tires screeched, sending up plumes of white smoke as they laid thick black tracks of rubber on the tarmac. It was then that I realized the front wheels were not in contact with the roadway—this crazy car was pulling a wheelie with street tires on it! I burst out in laughter like a child on a roller coaster. I definitely had to buy this car.

Ken eased back on the gas as the front end came down and bounced slightly. When I finally stopped laughing, Ken admonished that he only did that to demonstrate the extraordinary power-to-weight ratio of the car: with a full tank it barely topped 1,800 pounds and the mill was easily putting out something in the neighborhood of 500 hp. He cautioned against doing too many wheelies, saying "They're kind of hard on the frame molding and you may develop stress cracks in the body filler." Sage advice, as I would find out later.

By this time we were pulling back into Ken's parking lot. As I unbuckled the five-point harness and exited the car, Liz asked how it rode. "It pulls wheelies—honest!" was the only response I gave her.

I negotiated with Ken, but he didn't budge on what he wanted for the car. I did get him to concede to paying the charges to flatbed the car back to New Jersey, however. I gave him a $1,000 deposit and told him I would FedEx the balance in the form of a cashier's check as soon as we got back to Jersey.

We dubbed the car Screaming Mimi, which was an expression my dear old mom used to use occasionally to describe outlandish things. And the moniker certainly fit this car.

Screaming Mimi arrived on Tuesday morning by flatbed carrier from Cape Cod. As much as we wanted to start cruising with it immediately, there were several things that had to be done for safety

ALL SOLD OUT: Artist Peter Tytla's photo montage of an old-time gas station is a remembrance of things past and days gone by. (Artwork © Peter Tytla)

DEUCE DUET: This glorious pair of '32 Fords illustrates how exquisite craftsmanship and a fine eye for design can result in truly stunning contemporary hot rods. The three-window coupe at the rear is a jewel with its smooth looks, whereas the slick hard-topped roadster owned by Mark Westrick offers an equally elegant style built with amazing craftsman-ship. While both rods are similar they still boast individuality—part of what makes hot rods so interest-ing. (Photograph © David Fetherston)

reasons and to avoid getting tickets. For starters, the brake lights had to be made functional. Ken had used an inline pressure switch from a Volkswagen for the brake lights rather than a mechanical switch, so wiring up this switch was my first task.

After jacking up the car and crawling under it on a creeper, I got my first taste of what working on this rod was going to be like. There were two wires hanging down by the switch and both were red. Now which one of these was going to be the hot wire? That was the riddle. I put a call in to Ken and left a mes-sage for him to call me back regarding the wiring. In the interim, I decided to trace the wires back to their source to see what the story was. When I got to the point of origin at the rocker switch panel I was surprised, to say the least. Lo and behold, all of the wires were red—not a black, white, or green one among them. This was going to be fun, indeed.

Ken called me back and explained that the rear-most wire was the ground and the front wire was the hot lead. I asked him why all of the wiring was red, and he said he had bought a 500-foot roll of the stuff at a military surplus auction for $5. A great

buy for him and a great headache for me.

OK, so now the brakelights were working. I came upon a "cyclops" LED third brake light in a J. C. Whitney catalog and decided that it would work in Mimi's rear window, so I ordered one and installed it. The LEDs danced back and forth similar to the lights on the hood of the Firebird on the old *Knight Rider* TV series. When the brakes were applied, the LEDs flashed in unison, and when the left or right turn signal was activated the left or right bank of the LEDs blinked appropriately.

Ah, yes—turn signals. The rears weren't a prob-lem, since it was just a matter of wiring up with the brakelights. The fronts, however, were something else. A little creative thinking produced the idea to use motorcycle turn signals, so a pair of signals from a 1978 Harley-Davidson Superglide were pressed into service and mounted on the billet stems that sup-ported the bug-eye headlights. The headlights, by the way, also had to be wired to make them functional.

Since the dragstrip doesn't usually have traffic jams, Ken didn't bother installing a horn on the car. A friend had an old *ah-oogah* horn that she donated

to the cause and I promptly mounted it and wired it up.

Then I came across a classified ad for "firefly" LED valvestem lights in a hot rod magazine, so I ordered four of them at something like $30 a pair. These were neat red LEDs that screwed right onto the valve stem, powered by a hearing-aid battery. When the car was in motion, they created a red streaking circle as each tire rotated, a really cool effect.

Liz saw an ad for flamed shorts in another magazine, so we ordered them as well. Crazy car, kookie clothes—it all goes together, right?

In the next few weeks I got to know the car intimately and I marveled at some of the ingenious things Ken had done in building it. For example, the steering knuckle was made from a Snap-On universal-joint socket welded onto the steering column. It was obvious that Ken saved money wherever he could while working on this project.

The firewall had a tunnel-like indentation to accommodate the distributor, and the ridged lines of this indentation looked vaguely familiar, but I couldn't quite put my finger on where I had seen something like it before. Then, one day, while working on the wiring in back of the dashboard, I noticed the words "Good to the Last Drop" on the convex side of the firewall indentation. Ken had used a Maxwell House coffee can to create the tunnel indentation for the distributor!

We enrolled as members in the National Street Rod Association (NSRA) and that was when I learned the distinction between a "hot rod" and "street rod." Hot rods were generally built for speed, which meant that their engines were souped up and things like fenders, hoods, running boards, and other nonessential items were taken off the cars in an effort to save weight, which, in turn, helped increase their speed. Conversely, a street rod is a modernized vintage automobile that was manufactured in or before 1948. Street rods are usually decorated with colorful paint, have plush interiors and modern features such as disc brakes, air conditioning, and more. Hence, while

the hot rod was built solely for speed, the street rod is built for looks, comfort, and performance. Based on those criteria, I'd say Screaming Mimi is more hot rod than street rod.

We joined a local car club and became gung-ho members, going to every cruise night and car show around, often five or six a week. Being members of this club (which shall remain nameless to protect the innocent) proved to be quite an experience. We never thought in our wildest dreams that we'd encounter so many "car people" who were missing so many teeth! Two of the other members, Ken and Roy, had full dentition and we naturally gravitated to them, forming fast and solid friendships with them and their wives. Without realizing it, we had become car nuts and, on the odd night when nothing was happening, we'd just jump in Screaming Mimi and go for a cruise by ourselves. We logged more than 7,500 miles the first year we owned the car.

Every fall there's a big collector car event held in Wildwood, New Jersey, that spans an entire weekend. Imagine, if you will, 10,000 rods and customs running willy-nilly twenty-four hours a day for three days straight. Burnout contests at 2 A.M., street races, and just plain hell-raising in general are the norm. The police are hard pressed just to prevent injuries among the revelers. It's certainly no time to write tickets, as the financial boost to the local merchants and motel owners is a welcome shot in the arm for this small town that relies heavily on the summer tourist trade. Naturally, we had to attend.

At the end of the Wildwood weekend, Liz and I were caught in a sudden torrential downpour while cruising home on Garden State Parkway. Mimi's windshield wipers are mostly ornamental and barely functional. However, I kept a bottle of Rain-X in the trunk for such an eventuality. With the Rain-X on, the rain just sheeted and rolled off the vertical windshield so there wasn't a visibility problem. So there we were, merrily barreling down the parkway at 60 mph kicking up thirty-foot rooster tails of water from each tire, much to the dismay of all of the vehicles in back of us, who were now keeping a respectable distance to avoid the spray.

As we neared the end of our first season as hot rodders, the weather soon got cold. I reluctantly prepped Mimi for winter and drove her into a cargo container trailer we purchased for just this purpose. During that first season, we made some good friends and we got together regularly during the winter months for dinner and Sunday brunches, recounting the fun we'd had and making plans for the spring when we would once again enjoy our rides.

That was almost a decade ago. We still have Screaming Mimi and still enjoy taking her out for a spin. We owe a lot to this crazy little Dodge coupe; she literally changed our lives and was responsible for us meeting several new people who became our closest and dearest friends. And that's really what rodding is all about, when you come right down to it.

Last Knight

By Chuck Klein

Chuck Klein boasts a varied resumé. He has served as a police officer, firefighter, and private investigator. He's an author with a wide range of books to his credit. And last but far from least, he's a hot rodder from way back when.

Chuck writes about his car days in his novel *Circa 1957*, a coming-of-age tale set during the birth of rock and roll and hot rodding. His short-story collection *The Way It Was* features nostalgic tales of hot rods and romance.

This story is from *The Way It Was,* and while it is fiction, it all rings true and may have happened to an old-time hot rodder you knew.

*In the beginning was Elvis and Smokey
the Everly's, Richie, and Fats
four-on-the-floor or three-on-the-tree
and Darling Come Softly To Me . . .*

The young man in his late teens pulled into the driveway, eager to show his father and great grandfather his latest acquisition, a '32 Ford. Almost at the same time a delivery man arrived with a package. Taking the carefully wrapped box, with the word "Fragile" stamped in red on all sides, into the library of the ancient Tudor-style house, he approached a much-older man seated in a leather wingback.

"Pop." Then a little louder, "Grandpa, come outside for a minute I want to show you my new car. It's got all the extras."

The old-timer knew cars. He had studied, and in some cases rubbed shoulders with, the best of the early engineers, customizers, and racers. Men with the immortalized names of Iskenderian, Duntov, Barris, Fangio, Vukovich . . .

After the ritualistic inspection of the male bonding medium, the two men returned to the den where the younger remembered the package. "I almost forgot, Pop, this came for you a little while ago."

"What is it, Sonny?" the old man asked, settling into his overstuffed chair.

"I don't know, Pop. It's from some law office back east and it sounds like it has liquid in it. You getting your Geritol by mail now?" the great grandson joked.

Staring at the proffered package the old man pushed back further into the cushions of the chair as if trying to distance himself from it. His mouth dropped open. "Oh my God," escaped in a barely audible, raspy whisper.

"Grandpa, what's wrong? Are you okay?" The young gentleman crossed the room to take this ancient man's hand and search his frightened stare. "What is it, Pop?"

As recollections of events, forever melded to the sentimental portions of his mind, were forced to the present, the grandfather's eyes soon began refocusing to a new intensity. "Get a couple of glasses and some ice, Sonny—and call your Dad in here. I've got a story to tell you."

A man with graying hair and his teenage son watched the grandfather, in his ninety-sixth year, carefully and ceremoniously unwrap the package. Inside, sealed and encased in a solid wood box with a glass front panel, was a bottle of whiskey. Attached to the outside of this shrine was a small brass hammer and a pouch. From this pouch he pulled a sheet of paper containing a list of names—names that had lines drawn through each, save one.

It was a long time ago that they had met for the last time, a sort of reunion and farewell to one of the members who had but a short time to live. Pretensions and pressures were checked at the door that night. Whatever problems they faced outside seemed far away and unimportant. Maybe it was seeing a "best" friend for the first time in two or three decades or just that deep feeling that only comes from the knowledge that to this group each truly belonged. They all knew that this assembly was just this night only and never again would they all

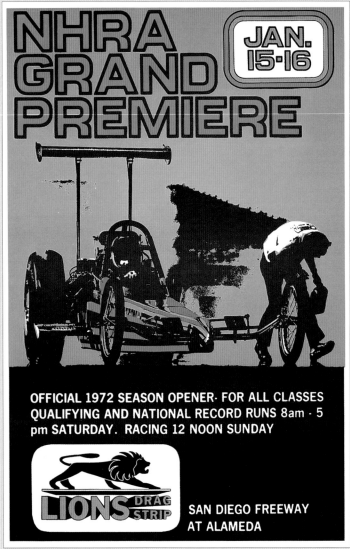

be together. Maybe it came with the understanding that these were their roots and the distinct sensation of having come home again. Perhaps it was the familiarity and companionship of old friends, whose dues were also paid in full. It was a most memorable occasion.

It wasn't a large gathering, but twenty-one men out of a possible thirty-six wasn't too bad for an informal reunion. Some had died, some couldn't be found, most were graying and pot bellied, but all had, at one time, belonged to the Knights of the Twentieth Century. Born so many years ago in a back-alley garage of a Midwestern American city, the Knights hot rod club was not unlike other clubs of guys of that era. Back when rock and roll was in its infancy and fast cars had to be built by hand, the members bonded together to learn, help each other, and talk engines, cars, and speed. It was exciting being the center of attention during this era of historic automotive and musical upheaval.

. . . Big Bopper and Ben E. King
and Love Is A Many Splendored Thing

"Here, you do it, Sonny," the old man said, handing the brass hammer to his grandson.

Uncapping the bottle, which had been freed by breaking the glass front, and without lifting his eyes from the list, the old man, in his articulate way, began to pour forth a tale as if he had been rehearsing it all his life.

"'Moonie,' that's what they called me because I was the first to have Moon wheel covers on my rod, a '34 roadster that I had stuffed a Caddy engine into. It had a dropped front axle, chopped windshield, and sported three-deuces on the engine. Though I never got it completely finished, it ran one-oh-three point six in the quarter mile. Not that this was the fastest in the club, but still very respectable. I didn't drive the roadster on the street much because something was always breaking, so I kept a stock '39 Ford as my everyday car. The '39 was battered and shabby and second gear was stripped but it ran quite reliably—those old Flatheads would just run forever. The only thing I hated about that old relic was the hot, scratchy mohair seats. I got my share of carpet burns on my elbow trying to put my arm around a girl.

"Ah, the girls. . . . It seems that we built and raced the cars to impress the girls and then whenever one of the guys had made enough of an impression, she'd up and marry him and that would be the end of his hot rodding. Brides and all the 'comes with' things

CLASSIC CUSTOM REBORN

Frank Livingston has built a number of exotic customs over the years. His '49 Chevy Fleetline fastback from the 1950s became one of the most famous mild customs of the era, winning the Oakland Roadster Show custom class in 1955, 1956, and 1957; appearing on two LP covers by The Deuce Coupes; and appearing as *Car Craft* feature car in June 1956 and on the cover in January 1958. Frank sold the Chevy years ago, thought again, and then built this clone of his famous old custom. Frank had Oz Welch at Oz's Customs do his new '49 Chevy and paintwork for him, swapping out the front glass for a one-piece Olds windscreen, adding '51 Kaiser taillights, smoothing the bumpers, and adding a '55 Plymouth grille. The rockers are molded into the skirts, the rear quarters flared and reformed, and the body painted in Pagan Gold with added diamond dust. The chassis uses a Mustang II front suspension, dropped spindles, and rack and pinion steering with the rear running de-leafed springs, blocks, Air Ride bags, and 15-inch chrome reversed wheels. Under the hood is '58 283 six and a three-speed manual transmission. The interior is traditional custom styling with pleated pearl white and pearl gold vinyl over vanilla wool carpets. (Photograph © David Fetherston)

associated with marriage probably contributed more to the demise of hot rodders and their clubs than anything else.

"You boys should have seen my bride! She was just about the prettiest thing that ever rode shotgun in an open roadster. I met her at a club dance—a 'sock hop,' we called it. She wore dungarees with the cuffs rolled up, in giant folds, almost to her knees. Her oversized shirt must have been her daddy's white dress button-down which also had huge folds of the sleeves all the way up her arm. The shirttails were tied in a knot at her tiny waist, the slightest view of smooth, soft skin barely visible. She wore her hair in a flip and she just had that fresh-scrubbed look about her. Quite the opposite of me with my axle-greased ducktails and form-fitted pink shirt with string tie and pleated slacks of charcoal gray. We rocked and rolled to the likes of Fats Domino, Dale Wright, Buddy Holly, and Larry Williams and when

she put her head under my chin to 'Sixteen Candles,' I knew it was something special. It was. Last week it would have been our seventy-second anniversary."

"Grandpa," the impatient teenager interrupted, "what about the bottle?"

"I'm comin' to that, Sonny. Don't rush me. Like I was saying, it was at this gathering when we all got together for that one last time to say goodbye to Freddie. Now, nothing lasts forever, and by age fifty Freddie had developed a terminal case of cancer. Knowing that he was a short timer he kept himself busy hunting us down and planning this assembly to unite us for one last time and to establish his gift as a tontine—the bottle from which we are drinking at this very moment. He said he won the fifth at a club dance and being a teetotaler, just put it away. Freddie was Jewish and for that solemn affair he gave us a little insight into these ancient teachings. It was such a somber and commemorative occasion that I

Right, top, **THE ROSE:** When the Barris Brothers built the famous Hirohata Mercury, custom cars took a new direction. The Merc was a turning point for folk searching for the perfect custom. To commemorate the creation of his first chopped Mercury and to honor the memory of his father, Sam Barris, John Barris convinced top custom car craftsmen and suppliers to donate their talents, funds, and materials to the building of this once-in-a-lifetime piece of automotive art for the Rose Tribute Foundation. Known as The Rose, this car was built in the Barris tradition of a fifties-style Merc custom but with current technology, including air suspension, billet wheels, and electronics. Mike Gray at Advanced Restoration in Sacramento did the vast majority of the car. The Rose combines a '48 Buick Sedanette roof with the Merc body to create a unique style. Finished in a gloriously rich coat of custom Rose Pink, a special color created by House of Color, it was built in just eight months with the help of Bill Novelli at Advanced Restoration. The Rose is powered by a highly detailed 351 Ford Lightening V8 and Ford ADO. (Photograph © David Fetherston)

Right, bottom, **BERT'S:** Customs and rods park outside Bert's late-night diner in this painting by Kent Bash. (Artwork © Kent Bash)

still remember his final words to us. Here was this dying compatriot, frail and weak, who looked each one of us in the eye as he decreed: 'In our faith it is believed that on Rosh Hashanah, the New Year, it is written; on Yom Kippur, The Day of Atonement, it is sealed:

How many shall pass on,
How many shall come to be,
Who shall live to see ripe age,
And who shall not,
Who shall live,
And who shall die;

and so it must be, that only the last surviving member of the Knights, the Knights of the Twentieth Century, may toast his fellow members with and savor the nectar of this, this last-man bottle.'"

With a sigh of finality, his still-steady hand—rough, dried and cracked like a cheap paint job that had crystallized—picked up the small doubles glass. Using both hands, and not unlike how one would make an offering, he raised the glass to just slightly above his head, whispering, "I'll see you soon fellas. Keep 'em tuned up."

Warmed by the energy of the aged whiskey the old man rose from the security of his wingback and shuffled to the leaded windows overlooking the springtime-embraced driveway. Just for an instant he was sure he saw Freddie waving from his '32 Ford, the one with the hopped-up Chevy engine and the plaque that said Knights, dangling from the back bumper. But, a deliberate wipe of the hand across his tear-filled eyes revealed it was only his grandson's brand-new '32 Ford.

The Roadster Chronicles:
The Tale of a Very Young Old Man
and His Very Old Young Car

By Budd Davisson

Budd Davisson likes things that are loud and fast. He's a pilot with a love for Pitts Specials and World War II warbirds. In addition, he's a fan of Pennsylvania long rifles and vintage Martin guitars.

His fascination with loud and fast dates back to his youth, when he built his first Model A roadster. Like many of us, Budd learned as he went and made do with what he could scrounge. That first roadster might not have made the cover of *Hot Rod,* but it was all his.

Budd recently uncovered his old roadster. The hot rod had become a time machine back to his own youth, as well as to the early days of hot rodding. This essay describes finding that piece of his teenage years and his subsequent work restoring—and redoing—his roadster.

EVEN A SMALL-TOWN KID CAN DREAM BIG . . .
Budding hot rodder Budd Davisson stands beside his creation circa 1958, wondering what to turn his torch to next. The headers made from an old bedstead were just one example of his handiwork. (Photograph © Budd Davisson)

I'm not certain why I'm writing this, but it seems important, if nothing else because the little car in question has been a part of my life, in one way or the other, for forty-seven years. I started it when fifteen years old, got it running a few years later, then it sat in my old shop in Nebraska for forty years before I retrieved it and brought it out here to Arizona, where I'm now bringing it back to its former non-glory. Not for one second of the intervening four decades was the car more than a millimeter from my heart.

Maybe the reason I feel compelled to tell you the ongoing story of this 1929 Model A roadster is just to show that there is such a thing as continuity in the universe. We're both, the car and I, survivors. We started life's journey together. I guess we'll end it together. May the circle, be unbroken, may the … you know the rest.

I'm not kidding you one bit when I say that this car *is* 1950s smalltown America. Through it I can smell the French fries, feel the sawdust on the gym floor under my stocking feet, hear the sound of dual pipes wrapping up between the cornfields, and remember so clearly what America was like when everything was right or wrong, black or white. It was cars and rock and roll and the hope you might get to first base before you graduated. Few of us seriously thought we'd actually get laid. We were all virgins in more

ways than one. Then the 1960s rolled around and took care of that in a hurry.

Those of us of the class of '60 are sort of schizophrenic because we were raised in the relative purity of the '50s, but then we were tasked with the mission of creating the furor that became the '60s. When I left high school I didn't know a single person who had even seen grass. When I left college and cleaned out my apartment, I found a half a brick of hash my roommate had misplaced. The changes were literally mind-bending, but through it all, the little roadster survived. And so did I.

EVEN A SMALLTOWN KID CAN DREAM BIG: A LITTLE HISTORY

When I was fifteen years old I decided I wanted a hot rod like those you saw in the pages of the California hot rod magazines like *Rod & Custom* (the little ones). To me, "California hot rod" meant only one thing: an open-wheeled roadster with no hood and a chromed engine. I can even tell you exactly where that desire came from: we had taken the train from my hometown in rural Nebraska to see my aunt in North Hollywood. The year was about 1951 and I was nine years old. We drove into the parking lot of the famous Brown Derby restaurant and, as we did, two black highboy roadsters pulled in next to us. I can

THE FOUNTAIN OF YOUTH FOUND: Budd Davisson's hot rod rediscovered in his family's quonset hut, more than four decades after he parked it. As Budd says of his find: "They say you can't go home again, but no one says you can't go out to the garage." (Photographs © Budd Davisson)

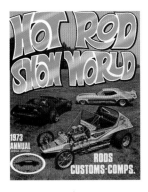

still feel the hair standing up on the back of my neck as I plastered my nose against the widow of our car. I was seriously hooked.

Even before I had a driver's license, I started looking for the elusive roadster body to make my hot rod out of. After a lot of backroad cruising with friends, I finally found a '29 Model A roadster body being used to stop erosion in a gully. Remember, this was 1957 and we're about thirty miles west of Lincoln, Nebraska. The average, perfectly drivable Model A Ford sold for $25, and this roadster was free for the taking.

Incidentally, getting a roadster body with a foot of mud in it out of a gully is no small feat, even with four young, strong backs. The body wasn't pretty. But it was mine.

The bits and pieces for the front end and driveline came from Marv Tobin's junkyard, which might as well have been Disneyland to me. I remember discovering and buying a V8-60 front axle, one of the round ones (oval actually), for $1.50; wiring it to the handle bars of my bicycle; and pedaling home with it. I was so proud I couldn't stand myself.

My father had forbid me to buy a "hot rod engine," meaning a Ford V-8, which was a potential problem. But not a big one.

In those days, when you were fifteen years old, you could get a driver's license to drive to school if you lived outside the district. Friends of mine had been driving a '39 Ford Tudor, which their father retired in favor of a later Chevy. I followed them down to Tobin's and lifted the engine out of the '39 while it was still warm. But then I had to get it home and couldn't use Dad's truck to do it. So a friend and I put the engine in a little wagon and pulled it home, more than two miles up and down hills. It was nearly a year before Dad found out I had that engine.

The bottom line is that the little car is now sitting in my shop and I'm hammering away on it knocking some of the crudeness off of it, but not deviating one iota from what the car was when I last drove it in 1962. I'm not going to replace anything with something newer unless it is something I personally fabricate and I'm not using a single reproduction piece. What homemade parts lack in finesse, they make up for in personality.

When I started the rebuilding process, I found, among other things, that I was an unbelievably crude craftsman when a teenager. For one thing, it looked as if I didn't own a drill because every hole was cut with a torch. The major stuff I had welded by the Vogel Brothers, but everything else I did and it looked as if I'd squeezed a sparrow and made him crap along the joint, the welds were so bad.

The historical circles in the car are wonderful. For instance, when I was building the car originally, there was a ten-year-old kid that hung around the shop for years, eventually growing into a teenager. He'd help me and I'd teach him what I knew—which turned out to be nothing, but we didn't know that at the time.

Flash ahead forty-two years: now that kid is the fifty-two-year-old proprietor of a one-man body shop that specializes in hot rods and antiques. I called Lowell Krueger up in Ashland, Nebraska, the day I exhumed the car and said, "Hey, Lowell, how'd you like to do the bodywork on my old roadster."

He answered, "I've been laying awake for forty years thinking about that car, knowing it was sitting in your old shed. Bring it on up."

Later, my good friend Dean Hillhouse, who hot rodded with me in high school, brought the car down to me in Arizona. He runs a radiator shop in Lincoln, just like his dad did. One day his shop manager looked at my old radiator and asked him, "Did you build this radiator?" and he said he didn't. His manager said, "Look at the patches. They are done exactly the same way you do them." Dean's dad had modified the radiator for me!

Because of the history in the car, I've decide that as much as possible, no one is going to work on it who didn't work on it the first time around and within practical limits, few parts will go on it that weren't on it when it was wheeled into the garage for the last time forty years ago. This includes stuff like the BT-13 Vultee airplane bucket seats and the over-the-frame headers made out of old bedsteads.

Folks, you want to see a 1950s hot rod? Well this is it!

They Say You Can't Go Home Again, But No One Says You Can't Go Out to the Garage.

ROADSTER RECOVERY

The cornfields along Highway 34 a few miles west of Lincoln sped past the Greyhound's windows. A familiar green monotony, they held no interest to

me, as my mind was somewhere else. Maybe I was streaking across El Mirage, pedal to the metal, a rooster tail of dust behind marking my roadster's way to a new record. Or maybe cruisin' Van Nuys Boulevard, where even guys like Von Dutch would notice my '29 lowboy.

As the bus made its way back to my small home-town, the images filled my sixteen-year-old mind and I fiddled nonstop with the various things that twisted and turned on the Offenhauser two-hole manifold sitting across my legs. After the first few miles, the other passengers stopped giving me odd looks. I became just a skinny kid with a ducktail who clung to the car part in his lap as if it were his Velveteen bunny.

I ignored them as I fondled, fiddled, and ma-nipulated my prize. The carburetors, the fabled 97s, weren't matched. One was chromed, one wasn't. But the air cleaners with the surrounding screen fes-tooned with punched-out holes that said "V-8" were almost like those I'd seen in the magazines, and the

locations in the magazines, the places with all the cool cars, was where part of me lived. That was the part that wanted desperately to have a car like those guys had. A true California hot rod roadster.

Only an hour earlier I'd been over at Speedway Motors, a modest store front on Lincoln's N Street, and a tall, easy-talking guy who introduced himself as Bill Smith had accepted my hard-earned $25 for the intake setup. He'd tossed in the polished fuel block for nothing.

Bill Smith had seen me often, as I'd take the bus from my hometown of 3,000 hard-working souls to the big city for the express purpose of looking at all the magical stuff hanging on the walls behind his counter and spread out around the shallow retail area. God, I can still smell the place in my mind! He even had one of those new Chevy V-8s dressed out in chrome and on a stand where we could all drool over it.

The pilgrimages to his tiny business wouldn't find me leaving with something tangible very often, but this time, I'd hit the jackpot. I had a dual carburetor intake. Now I was a real hot rodder!

Looking back at that time from the other end of history's telescope, I can see myself now as others must have seen me: a typical smalltown kid trying to be like those he saw in the magazines, sitting in a bus in rural Nebraska with a used, but very much loved, dual-carb setup in my lap.

Now, flash ahead forty-two years and it's July 4th weekend on the first year of the new millennium. I had carefully picked my way through the junk towards the back of the small Quonset hut that used to be part of my father's hatchery (on a hot day you can still smell the chickens).

Even throwing the side door open couldn't break the vague darkness that had settled on the place where I had spent some of my happiest years building things that ran (sort of, anyway). The narrow shaft of light revealed dark-primered metal and familiar curves. Even through the cobwebs and dust, the not-quite-dead shine of a pair of bonnet air cleaners broke through the gloom. Then came the ribbed reflection that I knew came from another Speedway acquisition, a set of Edmunds hi-comp heads.

My wife, the Arizona Redhead, asked from behind, "What can you see."

For a second, Howard Carter, the gentleman who discovered Tutankhamen's tomb, flashed across my mind. When peering through a hole into the tomb, he was asked the exact same question, and I answered the Redhead with his words. What did I see? I answered, "Things. Wonderful things!"

I had come full circle to the place where it had all begun. The roadster sat there, layered with miscellaneous junk, the tires becoming one with the pavement. The windshield was still broken where Jay Cattle had hit it when launched from his seat while the roadster vaulted over a curb. Craig Colburn, wanting to see how fast he could make it around the little traffic circle in the Hughes Addition, had pulled the steering wheel off in his lap and wound up in Bud Yerk's front yard. I'd forgotten to tell him I'd never put the steering wheel nut back on the old Ross steering column.

The over-the-frame headers, made from cut-up bedsteads, hadn't rusted through the silver paint, which surprised me. The bucket seats, from a dead Vultee BT-13 WWII trainer, were still there, the cushions being nothing more than the bottoms from seats stripped out of the Rivoli movie theater when it was rebuilt. The '40 dash still stared back through blind eyes because I never did get around to cutting the holes and installing a speedometer. Or any other gauge, for that matter.

Gauges weren't needed. You knew you were going too fast when you got scared. You knew the generator

HI-BOYS: In this painting by automotive artist Dale Klee, grass grows around two Hi-Boys in front of a forgotten gas station. (Artwork © Dale Klee)

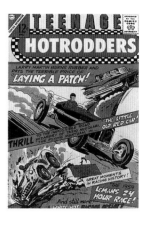

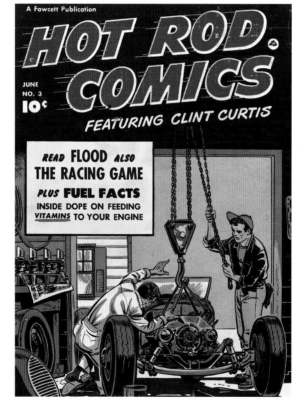

This page, clockwise from top left, **HOT RODS AND RACING CARS, VOL. 12, NO. 17, 1964**

HOT RODS AND RACING CARS, VOL. 1, NO. 9, APRIL 1953

TEENAGE HOTRODDERS, APRIL 1966

HOT ROD COMICS, VOL. 1, NO. 3, JUNE 1952

HOT ROD AND SPEEDWAY COMICS, SEPTEMBER–OCTOBER 1952

Facing page, **"HOT ROD" KING, VOL. 1, NO. 1, FALL 1952**

wasn't working when the lights went out. You knew the '39 V-8 Ford was hot (which was always—there was no fan) when vapor started blowing past your squinting eyes. You knew you were out of gas when you were coasting silently toward the curb.

I crawled over the top of the unbelievably dirty car to see it from the front. I couldn't walk around it because my '29 mail truck was squeezing it against the wall. In fact, there was so much car-related junk scattered around it, it was impossible to find a space on the floor to stand. I had to pick my way from this teetering '40 Ford rim to that rusty can of paint and so forth, like crossing a rock-strewn shallow stream.

Around up front, I found the shortened '34 truck shell covering the '40 radiator. I glanced around, searching. Yes, there it was, hanging on the wall where I had left it forty years earlier. There was the $10 deuce grille shell my cousin had secretly sold me at Speedy Bill's place. "Hey, Budd, I'm giving you a *really* good deal on this—*ssshhhh!*"

Exhuming the car was a trip in itself. For one thing, it was totally surrounded and covered by old cream cans and other miscellaneous junk. The tires had turned to concrete and those on the left side had molded themselves into the drain gutter that ran around the floor.

Throwing a chain around the rear axle to the drawbar on our little Farmall Cub tractor (1953 and still in use), I started tugging. I was moving along at a pretty good clip when suddenly the car stopped as solidly as if I'd shoved a screwdriver into the gears. *Bam!* The tractor died and I just knew something important in the old roadster had locked up. Major headache!

"No problem," Dean said, "All four tires just came around and hit the flat spot at the same time."

Take a note: petrified tires don't roll, even when hooked to a tractor.

A funny side note: just as we were preparing to change the tires for rollers, Dean decided to try putting air in them. I openly scoffed. But not for long. Not only did they blow up perfectly but the rears were the tubeless snow tires off my folk's station wagon and they held air with no leaks. This despite the cracks going through the sidewalls where they'd been folded. The tires stayed on the car all the way through the rebuild. Go figure.

When the car rejoined me recently and we rolled it into the garage, I immediately threw a leg over the door and dropped into the dirty seat. I was home again! And so was the old car. It had a *long* way to go, but we'd done it once before and we could do it again.

For the next few weeks, I'd periodically pad out to the garage in my stocking feet before going to bed, turn on the lights, take a long look, then turn, and retrace my steps. I just couldn't believe. The roadster was actually back in my life.

FRAMED

As I began to rebuild the car, I was continually running into the old me—and many times I didn't like that me. Not as a craftsman anyway. On the one hand, I was amazed that I'd had the arrogance as a fifteen- and sixteen-year-old kid to think I could actually build a car from scratch. And I'd puff up in pride. Then I'd look at the unbelievably bad worksmanship and think, "Do I really want to recreate this thing the way I did it then?"

The frame, for instance, turned out to be an interesting saga that was unnecessarily complicated by what started out as an unreasoning desire to keep this thing "exactly as I did it in high school."

First of all, what I did in high school redefined the word "crude" and added new meaning to "butchery."

As a kid, from the beginning I knew I wanted this sucker low and sneaky like some of the magazine cars. That meant channeling the body, which has nothing to do with the frame, but "low" also meant getting the frame closer to the ground. At the rear that meant somehow kicking up the frame so the rear crossmember sat higher. In the front, that would normally have meant a dropped axle. That decision, however, was complicated by the '40 Ford V8-60 front axle that was my prize possession. For a time it even stood in the corner of my bedroom.

I don't remember what a dropped axle cost in those days, probably about $20 used, which I could have scrounged up somehow, but I was determined to use that round axle. That decision complicated the living hell out of everything I did on the front of the frame—the radiator size and placement, spring suspension, grille shell attachment, and on and on.

To get the frame down in front, I ran the spring over the top of the suicide spring perch, thereby gaining another 2½-inch drop because the car hung from the bottom of the spring rather than sitting on top.

But the frame *still* didn't sit low enough for me. Forget that we had railroad tracks all over town and the driveway to my house had a big dip in it, I wanted this thing L-O-W. So, I cut the front of the frame and

Z'd it, stepping it up and gaining another 4 inches of drop. Now it was LOW!

All of this took place *after* I had the body channeled down over the frame (welded in place) *and* the engine mounts welded in. When I dropped the engine back in after cutting and Z'ing the frame, I found I could bounce the oil pan off the garage floor by jumping up and down on the front of the frame. Well, at least it was low. Back to the drawing board. The engine had to be raised.

To make a long story short (too late, right?), I wound up with the back of a Willys frame of some kind brazed/welded/bolted to the back of the frame to kick it up. The front spring perch was hacked out of ¼-inch plate with a torch and the spring holes burned in it. To mount the Ross steering box (that was the hot setup according to the little *Rod & Custom*), I torched a big chunk out of the left frame rail flange and did my version of welding a plate in to mount it and, again, burned the mount holes in it. Yessir, this kid was born to be a jeweler.

So, now it's four decades later and this crippled-looking frame is sitting on my shop floor in Arizona and I'm determined to save it in the interest of historical accuracy. In the interest of brevity, let's just say that six months, an entire roll of MIG wire, and lots of steel plate later, what I had was this twisted, out-of-square frame that was much stronger but still incredibly ugly. I just knew people were going to walk away thinking that's the kind of craftsman I am. That one thought kept circling in my brain and became a searing, psychic sore.

One day, as I was sitting on a stool staring at this monstrosity, I calmly got up, fired up the cutting torch and proceeded to whack the rear crossmember off the frame and excise the '37 motor mount member from the front. In fifteen minutes, all of that work and all of the history was a pile of scrap behind my shop, the cut ends still smoldering. I had finally found the only proper use of a cutting torch in hot rodding.

In less than two months I had fabricated a new frame. It's straight, clean, and looks like the frame my teenage mind envisioned but my teenage hands couldn't craft.

So, now, when I look at the frame I see the original crossmembers from my teenage years combined with more than forty years of new experience. I

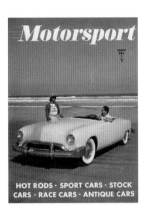

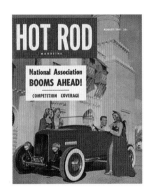

guess you might say I'm building it as I would have as a teenager if I had known then what I know now. I don't think that's going too far astray from the concept, do you?

MAGICAL MOMENTS

As I was grinding away on that frame, I had moments of déjà vu that were so strong I had to stop, lean back, and enjoy them. Most had to do with the delicious continuity provided by old songs. The Beach Boys launched into "409" and I flashed back to when I heard it for the first time over my shop radio as a kid. Here I was, well past middle age, working on the same car, using the same tools, listening to the same songs. There's a connection there that can't be explained to those who don't instantly understand it. On the other hand, it might just be a record-setting case of arrested development.

The tools aren't just tools and the car isn't just a car. These are tangible pieces of my youth that keep reaching out to let me know that the hair may be going gray, but the spirit is still in there rockin' and rollin'.

"I HAVE TO LIVE IN THIS TOWN!"

Looking back, it's obvious that being young, with a world that only extended as far as the newsstand and the cornfield past that, it's not always logical what sticks in your mind as being cool and necessary. But then, logic has never had much to do with hot rods, while cool is a prime ingredient.

Dad took me to see sprint car races when I was about fourteen and for some reason, the shape of their exhausts struck me as being unbelievably beautiful. The flowing lines from which horsepower galloped at higher-then-human decibels were, to me, the very embodiment of speed. Anything that was going to go fast or, more important to me at the time, was going to look as if it went fast, had to have headers like that. Even as a teenager I knew it was all in the presentation. You gotta look good.

One of the identifying characteristics of being from a rural farming community is that you don't look much further than your own scrap pile when you start building something. In this case, Dad had a bunch of old bedsteads out in back of the store and it never once entered my mind to go down to Keller's in town and buy some exhaust tubing.

In those days I was great on concept but more than a little short in the execution area. I started hacking at the tubing (I had lots to work with) with the torch and was satisfied if the gaps were less than a ¼-inch wide. I'd gotten pretty good at globbing brazing rod into big gaps so I wasn't too concerned about exact fit. Actually, that statement pretty much described the entire car! Exactitude wasn't much in evidence anywhere.

Before long, I had the over-the-frame sprint car headers I wanted and they definitely had the look, if not the detail. And they had the desired effect. They looked fast. They sounded fast. And they were guaranteed to get me in trouble.

One of my fondest memories is my dad stepping out of the lilac bushes into the middle of the street late one night to flag me down. I had been running up and down Hillcrest Drive in front of the house, headers uncapped, looking down over the door every time I backed off the gas and grinning at the flames shooting out of the stacks.

Dad was not grinning. He said, "I have to live in this town. Get that thing off the street—*now!*"

I was to hear the "I have to live in this town" speech on a regular basis as I grew older and found even more obtuse ways to embarrass him. He saw me as an alien dropped into his small town and what we were experiencing wasn't a generation gap. It was a species gap.

That was then. This is now.

In the forty-four intervening years, I haven't come up with a better-looking design for headers. I still love midgets and sprints and their exhaust systems still turn me on.

I have to be honest: I did lots and lots of welding and patching and put new flanges on the old headers. In the end, however, I found they were paper thin (bedsteads aren't built for cruising down the street). In regular use, their life span would have been measured in hours.

I had already built the new frame, so I'd pretty much trashed the gotta-be-as-it-was-in-high-school rule and the headers were the next move. Still, the new headers had to look exactly like the old ones. Only better.

The problem was that the bedsteads were bent on a 7-inch radius, which is what gave them that swoopy, art deco look, and the closest I could come

GEE BEE HOT ROD:

Geoff Mitford-Taylor based his Deuce roadster on the 1930s R-1 Gee Bee air racers. The Gee Bee was all engine with just minimal wings, making it a handful to fly; even so, famed pilot Jimmy Doolittle won the Thompson Trophy Race at the stick of a Gee Bee. For Geoff, his roadster was a tribute to the daring flyers who risked all in the pursuit of performance. In some respects, it's not a fancy rod, but then that's not what Geoff was after. He built it on a stock '32 frame, which he boxed, adding new crossmembers, a '57 Ford 9-inch rear axle, and a Super Bell dropped front axle. Power comes from a stock 350 Chevy V8. The body is a Wescott's fiberglass replica finished in red and white, with gracefully curving graphics mirroring the Gee Bee. The interior is racer simple, with wooden seats modeled after the Spruce Goose atop hand-fabricated metal floor and side panels. Other neat touches include the 15-inch wire wheels and the ultra-rare ECJ headlights. (Photograph © David Fetherston)

were 3-inch bends. Then one morning at 3 A.M., it hit me. I leaped out of bed and started leafing through the yellow pages. Then I paced around the house for about five hours waiting for people to get to work so I could call them.

People seem so inefficient when it's 4 A.M. and they aren't answering their phones at work yet. Lazy bastards!

Finally the doors opened for business and I made the call.

The voice said, "Arizona Four-Wheeler." In less than three minutes, my problems were solved. They built tubing chassis and could bend anything. When I picked up the tubing, I was delirious. It was perfect!

Am I happy with the final result? Absolutely. I still can't keep myself from grinning when I look at them. I definitely got the look I was after and they are so close to the originals you'd have to measure them to tell the difference. That is, you can't tell the difference if you ignore the glaring difference in detail work.

I know the first time I fire up that engine I'm going to hear a voice in the distance, "I have to live in this town." This time, however, everyone will know it's me, the past-middle-aged guy next door, ripping back and forth at night with no father to reel him in. Pity!

GHOST OF DRAGSTRIP HOLLOW, 1959

THE CHOPPERS, 1962

JOY RIDE, 1958

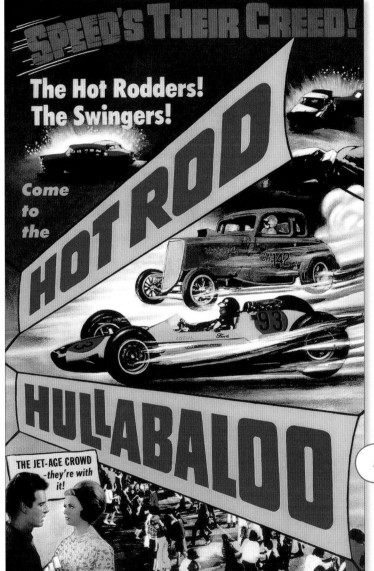

BIKINI BEACH, 1964

HOT ROD HULLABALOO, 1966

THE WILD RIDE, 1960

MERC MASTERPIECE:
When the Ayala and Barris brothers began chopping '49 Mercs all those years ago, little did they imagine that the custom world would look back on them as modern-age Michelangelos in metal. The style they set has not yet been outdone—and perhaps never will. Marvin Giambastiani has been meddling with customs since the early 1960s and always wanted a chopped Mercury. His Merc was chopped 4 inches by Jerry Covin at Pilgrim Auto Body in Santa Rosa, California. Marv performed the usual tricks, including shaved doorhandles and trim, frenched headlights, and black paintwork. It was later repainted pearl fuchsia for an all-round cool ride. (Photograph © David Fetherston)

Clockwise from left,
THE SHAGGY DOG'S ROADSTER

THE MONKEES' MON-KEEMOBILE

PSYCH-OUT'S VOX-MOBILE

THE MUNSTERS' MUNSTER KOACH

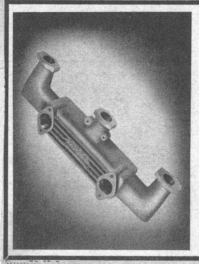